UNDERSTANDING LITERACY DEVELOPMENT

Peter Geekie, Brian Cambourne
and Phil Fitzsimmons

Trentham Books

First published in 1999 by Trentham Books Limited

Trentham Books Limited
Westview House
734 London Road
Oakhill
Stoke on Trent
Staffordshire
England ST4 5NP

British Cataloguing in Publication Data
A catalogue record for this book is available from the
British Library
ISBN 1 85856 086 1

Designed and typeset by Trentham Print Design Ltd., Chester and
printed in Great Britain by Bell & Bain Ltd., Glasgow

Contents

This book is dedicated to Bill who loved to read and Ivy who loved children.

Acknowledgements

This book could not have been written without access to the classrooms of Rhonda Fisher, Hazel Brown and Ruth Geekie. These outstanding teachers enriched our understanding of literacy instruction both by allowing us to observe them as they taught and by offering insightful comments on the children's learning. We benefited enormously from their intelligence and experience. We offer them our profound gratitude for their generosity and tolerance.

We are also indebted to Leslie Jordan, Julie Winkler and Robert and Carol Garner who told us about their children. Parents like these are the best teachers of all.

Peter Keeble and Bridie Raban read the text and made comments. We value both their suggestions for the improvement of this book and their friendship over many years.

We acknowledge the children themselves. They never failed to surprise and delight us. Time spent in the company of children is never time wasted. We thank them all.

Finally we wish to thank our families whose experience of being peripherally involved in the writing of this book did not always bring them joy. Without their patience and support the text could not have been completed.

Key to data transcriptions

In Chapters 1 to 6 extracts from videotaped data are extensively used. The objective was not to produce an analysis of linguistic data but to represent the talk as accurately as possible while simultaneously making it easy to read and comprehensible. The transcription code is as follows

Normal use of question marks and exclamation marks is maintained.

*   pause of one second or less

**   pause of less then 2 seconds but more than 1 second

***   pause of less than 3 seconds but more than 2 seconds

Bold type   emphatic speech

CAPITAL LETTERS indicates that the speaker is using letter names

C-O-M-E   indicates that the speaker is spelling the word using letter names.

No capital letters or full stops are used for direct speech but normal punctuation is used for any comments or additional details.

When either teacher or child engages in phonemic segmentation of a word an attempt has been made to indicate the type of sound produced but no attempt has been made to record the phonemes accurately.

Chapter I

We were struck by the number of participants at a recent conference who referred to 'the psychological model' of reading. Psychology has many faces and there are significant differences between psychologists about the nature of learning. What was said about reading implied assumptions about learning which were not challenged, except by us. Unfortunately this is usually what happens in debates about literacy development and instruction. Disagreements about different 'methods' of teaching imply differences in beliefs about how children learn which are rarely made explicit.

The so-called 'psychological model' of reading is based on research which assumes that the human mind, like the computer, is essentially an asocial processor of information. According to this view the brain receives information from the environment through the senses, encodes it, stores it in memory and retrieves it, when it is needed, to make sense of daily experience or to solve problems. Research done by psychologists within this information processing paradigm has long established that the human brain is limited in its capacity to process information, but different information processing theories explain in different ways how those limitations are overcome during reading. Top-down theorists propose that reading is meaning-driven. Information stored in long-term memory allows print to be processed in large meaningful chunks. Reading problems occur, these theorists say, when the reader tries to process small, meaningless units of information which clog the short term memory and prevent the reader from maintaining a focus on meaning.

Bottom-up theorists, by contrast, say that it is the development of automaticity that helps the reader to overcome processing limitations.

While skilled readers might pay relatively little attention to grapho-phonemic relationships and focus on meaning in their responses to printed language, beginning readers (according to this view) must first learn to deal with grapho-phonemic correspondences and develop automatic 'decoding' responses to the visual patterns of words. Practice in word recognition leads to automatic access to word meanings, and when word meanings can be retrieved automatically children can give their attention to the higher level processes required to understand written language.

One practical expression of such a view of reading development is found in the critique by Roger Beard and Jane Oakhill (1994) of Liz Waterland's *Read With Me*. This critique was written because of the concern the authors felt about the influence of Waterland's monograph which, amongst other things, suggested that the capacity to use phonic clues to recognise words develops out of the child's experience of reading, rather than being the product of instruction. Beard and Oakhill see the matter differently. According to them reading is '... a series of skills, fluently used, though the component skills, since they are so automatic and well-integrated in skilled readers, may be difficult to discern' (p.19). Those skills can and must, nevertheless, be identified and taught to beginning readers. In this instructional process the teacher is the adult expert, and children learn by being shown and told. The child is the novice who learns to master the skills through explicit instruction and repeated practice.

The vast majority of children, we are told, don't just 'pick up' the rules of the writing system. They learn to read because they are taught. Systematic and explicit instruction in phonics and the 'accompanying skills of segmenting and blending words' is necessary if children are to become independent readers. Beard and Oakhill go on to cite a sequence of exercise types which will help to develop 'a working knowledge of the structure of words' so that children can read unfamiliar words and not be forced to rely on guessing with the help of context. Skilled readers, they say, do not skip or ignore words or letters. In fact, they '... process them very thoroughly, but very automatically, so that the processes involved in word recognition do not interfere with their comprehension'. It is only the rank beginner, and the backward reader, who makes extensive use of context.

Beard and Oakhill are doing much more than discussing reading instruction. Implicit in what they have to say is not just a set of beliefs about reading but also sets of beliefs about knowledge, the relationship between learning and instruction, and the nature of children's minds. It is clear that they believe that learning involves a transmission of knowledge and skills from teacher to learner, with the teacher determining what is to be learnt, and in what order. And what is being learnt is a set of skills, demonstrated by an expert, and mastered through repeated practice of the component skills.

This book has been written in response to positions like the one adopted by Beard and Oakhill which are based on the so-called 'psychological model of reading', because not all psychologists work within the information processing paradigm. In this chapter we will review research studies which present an account of learning which is very different from the one upon which Beard and Oakhill base their 'more balanced approach' to reading instruction. This research was done by a group of developmental psychologists who do not accept that learning is something done in isolation from other human beings. They do not accept the proposition that learning can be best understood if we start with the assumption that the human mind is essentially a processor of information. Instead they assume that children are social beings constantly engaged with other people in making sense of their world of experience. Learning, from this perspective, is social and collaborative in nature. Such a view of learning is much more useful in trying to make sense of literacy development than the model which information processing psychologists offer us.

Talking and Learning

Because learning is social and collaborative, and because it happens all the time, not just in classrooms and psychological laboratories, the authors often find themselves listening in to conversations between adults and children in various public places, and almost always the talk involves learning. Meanings are negotiated. The child fine-tunes his or her understanding of the world in one way or another. And at the end of the conversation the shared understandings of adult and child overlap more than they did at the beginning. Here is an example of one such conversation.

A father and his five year old son are in a train travelling along a coastal stretch of track south of Sydney. The train passes under a wide bridge.

'It's a tunnel,' the child exclaims.

'No,' says the father. 'It's a bridge.'

Several miles further along the father looks out the window of the carriage along the curve of the track, anticipating a long tunnel. He looks back to his child, makes eye contact and then looks out of the window again.

'Look,' he says, turning to the little boy again, 'here comes a tunnel.'

He points ahead. The child looks out of the window and then back at his father.

'It's very soon,' the father says, leaning back in his seat so that he can see along the track. The child shifts his position so that he can see out of the window too.

'Can you see?' the father asks. 'Can you see the tunnel? Here it comes. Here comes the tunnel.'

They are both looking out the window now at the approaching tunnel. As the train enters the tunnel the father turns to his son.

'We're in the tunnel now.'

He looks out the window again and then back at his son.

'There's the tunnel walls,' he says, nodding in their direction.

Then he looks out of the window again and the little boy follows his gaze again. They turn to each other and make eye contact.

'It's very dark,' says the father.

He looks out the window again and points. He turns back to his son, still pointing.

'And there's the end.' he says. He looks out the window and points again. The child looks in the direction indicated. 'You can see the end coming.'

The train bursts out into the sunlight. The father smiles at his son.

'That was a big one,' he says.

Thirty minutes later the train reaches a large city station which has a shopping complex built in the air space above it. Light conditions are subdued. The child looks out the window and then back at his father.

'Is this a tunnel?' he says.

A good question. The father considers his answer.

'No,' he says. 'It's a bit like a bridge.'

There is nothing exceptional about this conversation. Every day, in every conceivable situation, children are learning through dialogue just like this little boy. As Frank Smith (1983) observed, learning isn't something that happens only when children are stimulated or reinforced. It goes on naturally and constantly as children and adults try to build a common basis of understanding through language.

Roger Brown (1980, pp.187-209) has remarked that adults learn about gaps in children's knowledge from conversational breakdowns. By maintaining communication with their children adults can check on children's progress in developing the mass of grammatical, semantic and pragmatic knowledge which they share with their families. This little boy's linguistic competence was impressive. His knowledge of grammar and pragmatics was evident in his ability to take part in various conversations during the trip. He knew how to make appropriate contributions at appropriate times in acceptably structured utterances. The 'breakdown' in this conversation was a matter of semantics. The child labelled a bridge inaccurately as a tunnel. This led to an attempt by the father to make the child's understanding of bridges more specific; more like his own.

The adult's decision to correct his child is, of course, crucial. With a younger child he might have let the labelling of the bridge as a tunnel pass without comment. But if he had not corrected his son there would have been no development of the child's understanding of the nature of tunnels as distinct from bridges. Obviously he had a concept of what a tunnel was before this series of exchanges began. Perhaps he had developed that understanding on the basis of observation, unassisted by anyone else. We cannot know the details of this. But we do know, in the situation we observed, that any growth in the child's understanding depended upon adult intervention and guidance. That is important.

Specifically, what is involved in this incident is the negotiation of reference; that is, how to use language to refer to specific things. In this case it is bridges and tunnels that are being referred to, and what is going on is the fine-tuning of the child's understanding of the distinction between them. When is something that might be a tunnel really a bridge? How can we know which labels to use so that our communicative intentions can be made clear to other people? This is a vital part of what is learnt in mastering a language, and it is fundamental to successful learning. If we do not share an understanding of which words, used by our conversational partners, refer to which objects or events, then there is no basis for the construction of mutual understanding.

There is, of course, a structure to referring (Bruner, 1983, pp.67-70). It is a structure that the little boy would have learnt earlier in his life, and he was assisted in learning about tunnels because his father used familiar means to achieve the intended purpose. In trying to make his child's understanding of tunnels more precise the father first established joint attention. He called on his son to look, using pointing and the direction of his gaze as further indications of what he was referring to. The child's attention was gained and he did indeed look where his father had indicated. This is a crucial step in the establishment of reference. As Bruner (1983) has pointed out, asymmetries in knowledge are to be expected in adult-child conversations. The father knows all about tunnels and the child knows little. Nevertheless, when joint attention has been established, a joint referent exists that 'can be developed both for its truth value and its definiteness'(p.68). As long as both parties to the conversation are focused on the same thing and communication continues, then it is possible that something closer to a mutual understanding will eventuate.

Because the train was moving and its relationship to the tunnel was constantly changing, maintaining a joint focus was not easy. The father was clearly aware of this and worked to sustain joint attention. When the train entered the tunnel, he marked this transition clearly. He established eye contact with the boy again and said, 'We're in the tunnel now.' The experience of the tunnel has changed but the father maintains the stability of its identity for the child. In fact, rather than just being an act of labelling, the conversation now makes the tunnel a topic; something to be commented upon. Implicitly the father is saying that this is a good example of what a tunnel is. What is being experienced has the features which distinguish tunnels from other phenomena, including bridges. The adult's comments ensure that the point is not missed. Not only is this what we call a tunnel. It is called a tunnel because it has walls, and is dark and long.

Most of what has been said about this incident so far has been about what the father did. But the adult's intervention, while necessary, was not sufficient. The growth of understanding depended upon the child's engagement in thinking about the distinction; and that engagement clearly took place, as we can see from his question about the status of the railway station under the shopping centre. This question is interesting in a number of ways. We've noted that this question would almost certainly never have been asked if the father had ignored his son's incorrect labelling of the railway bridge. Instead he attempted to increase the exactness of the child's understanding of tunnels as they contrast with bridges. In other words, prerequisites to learning seem to have been

1. that the child was made aware of a deficiency in his capacity to refer accurately to tunnels

2. the provision of a model of a tunnel which he could use as a standard for making future judgements about things that might be called tunnels.

If our observations had stopped here, however, it would have been impossible to know whether the child had actually learnt anything from his father. It was the problematic status of the station under the shopping centre that apparently prompted the child's question and made it apparent that he was actively engaged in refining his capacity to refer conventionally to tunnels. According to laboratory-based research, children under seven typically have problems with the recognition of verbal ambiguity and rarely ask clarifying questions. But here in the actual world of conversation between parents and children about the world which surrounds them, this child seems not only to be aware of ambiguity but also seeking to resolve it by asking a question. It does not matter that the father cannot categorise this phenomenon; a station under a shopping centre. It is neither bridge nor tunnel. There is no word yet that precisely labels this aspect of our reality. But perhaps part of what was learnt was that sometimes referring is a difficult process which might not always be successfully achieved. It might require further thought, experience and negotiation before understanding is fully achieved.

Another matter of interest to us as we observed this interaction was the way both adult and child took for granted the text of the prior conversation. Perhaps fifteen minutes passed between the child's initial incorrect labelling of the bridge and the act of reference to the tunnel, but the father did not refer explicitly to the earlier incident to provide a context for understanding. Implicit in the conversation was the expectation that the child would *remember* that he had called a bridge a tunnel. If he could not recall that earlier exchange, his father's current comments would surely make little sense to him. Another half hour then passed without further reference to tunnels and bridges, although the train passed under a number of bridges. The child's question, 'Is this a tunnel?' shows that his father's assumption was not misplaced. He had linked the two occasions and was now making a further connection. And in asking the question he is assuming that his father also remembers their previous exchanges about tunnels and bridges. The learning conversation has as its topic what has been foregrounded in the current situation (the station under the shopping centre) but it assumes a common, remembered background of experience, and a capacity to refer to that common experience. This is of great importance in understanding the ways in which classroom talk contributes to learning, including learning about literacy.

The general significance of this incident should not be overlooked. Whatever the child knew about tunnels before, and whether or not that knowledge had been acquired through his independent exploration of the world, there would seem to be little doubt that any increase in his understanding of the nature of tunnels was dependent on social interaction. The adult responded to the child's inappropriate label, established joint attention on an example of a tunnel, labelled it and then specified its attributes by commenting on it. Later the child, confronted by a problematic case, asked a question designed to further clarify his understanding. Both parent and child responded to the other, and some progress seems to have been made towards a shared understanding of the nature of tunnels. The same process can be observed in classrooms when the labels are in written language and even when the act of referring is directed at language itself rather than objects and people. What matters is that the child has developed control over the social processes that permit the negotiation of agreement about the meanings of things. It is through the use of these social processes that learning proceeds.

So it can be seen that the learning process is essentially social, but *what* is learnt is cultural in nature. Lev Vygotsky said that human learning '... presupposes a specific social nature and a process by which children grow into the intellectual life of those around them'(Vygotsky, 1978, p.88). It is cultural as well. Children learn to see the world through the eyes provided by their culture; perhaps a culture in which the distinction between bridges and tunnels is significant. It is not just categories and labels which are learnt but also learn culturally specific ways of communicating and thinking and solving problems.

The critical feature of social interaction in Vygotsky's theory is that it is *a shared thinking process* during which the support of an expert is available to the learning child (Rogoff, 1990, p.192). This is what is involved in the above episode. The child is learning how his father labels aspects of the world. And his father is teaching his son the meanings used by his culture. The means by which this is achieved is that the father ensures that he and his son establish a focus on the same thing and then talk about it. Consciousness is shared. The child is not just learning a label but is learning how to participate in the way his culture thinks about things.

This brings us to Vygotsky's view of the relationship between learning and development. Vygotskian theory proposes that learning precedes and promotes mental development. Instruction should therefore identify those tasks which children cannot manage alone but can complete with assistance. If these 'ripening' functions are identified and developed through instruction, mental development is promoted. Our experience as researchers has provided data which support this view of the relationship between learning and development. For example, five-year-old children who were unable to read or write independently have produced written texts with assistance, and have been able to read them back. This capacity to engage in such acts of 'shared thinking' proved to be an indicator of future literacy development.

In summary, then, we believe the little boy in the anecdote, like all children, is actively engaged in interpreting his world. But he needs the support of his father; someone more knowledgeable than he is. What children learn is essentially what their culture offers them, through the intervention of others. It is a feature of human society that knowledge is passed down from generation to generation. The adults who instruct children help them to acquire this pre-existing cultural knowledge. And this is done, not by transferring knowledge from mind to mind, but through collaborative sessions in which the children participate in acts of shared thinking with someone more competent than themselves.

Learning as puzzle solving

No theory is ever complete and Vygotsky's explanations of learning and development have been elaborated and developed in a number of significant research studies in the last twenty years. Accounts of learning have been built on a Vygotskian foundation by such researchers as Jerome Bruner, David Wood and Barbara Rogoff. These people are participants in what has been called 'a quiet revolution' in developmental psychology, a revolution involves the recognition of children as social beings who, through social interaction, '...acquire a framework for interpreting experience, and learn how to negotiate meaning in a manner congruent with the requirements of the culture' (Bruner and Haste, 1987, p.1). As a way of discussing some of the insights into the nature of learning offered by these and other researchers, we turn again to an example taken from informal observations of adults and children interacting in natural settings.

> Liam is the grandson of one of the authors. During visits to his daughter's home Peter was struck by how closely the exchange between his daughter and her child paralleled the behaviour of mothers in formal research studies. It will be used for that very reason: because it demonstrates that the best theoretical accounts of learning and instruction are those which can be validated by reference to what real people do in natural contexts.

> One present Liam received on his third birthday was a jigsaw puzzle of a fire engine. One fireman was at the steering wheel talking on a telephone. Another was uncoiling a large hose. Others were climbing out of the cabin onto the street.

> When Jacqui, his mother, first sat down with him to do the puzzle she tried to use the picture on the puzzle box as a guide but this proved to be of no use. Liam clearly did not understand the nature of the task. He was unable to connect the picture with the puzzle. So she decided to try to do a section at a time.

The ladder on top of the fire engine was a prominent feature of the puzzle, occupying about a quarter of its total area, so she started there. As she handled the pieces she talked about them.

'Let's find all the ladder pieces. Is this a bit with the ladder on it? All right, let's find another one. What about this one? It's got ladder on it. And that looks like a fireman's hat. See? Let's see if they go together. Here. Help me put them together. I'll hold this piece while you push the other one. That's right.'

She did most of the work, getting Liam to 'help' find pieces of the puzzle and put them together. She worked down the puzzle following the same routine with each section of it. The pieces with parts of the hose on them. The pieces with the number plate. The pieces with parts of the wheels. She talked about them, saying what they were, pointing to the identifying features of each piece, showing how the features of one piece matched with features of its neighbouring pieces, and coercing Liam's assistance in putting them into place.

When the puzzle was finished Jacqui discussed the picture with Liam, looking at the picture as a whole rather than as an assemblage of parts.

'Look Liam, that man is driving isn't he? And he's talking on the telephone too. Can you see him? And can you see the men walking down the steps? Show me where they are.'

And so on.

They did the puzzle again. And again the next day. Soon Liam became a more active partner in the activity. It wasn't long before he was doing most of the puzzle himself while his mother watched, guiding him with clues and cues when he seemed unable to go on by himself.

'You need a piece with the hose on it. Can you see one. Is that it? Does it fit? Well, see if you can find another one with the hose on it.'

And Liam started to ask questions.

'Mummy, does this piece go here?'

In a surprisingly short time he was able to do it himself with almost no assistance. And he talked to himself as he did it. At first he used the cues provided by his mother.

'There's another piece of ladder. Does this go here?'

He joined the piece of puzzle successfully to a neighbouring piece.

'Here's the man with the telephone. '

He put this piece into position and looked at his mother.

'Is that right?' he asked. Jacqui nodded.

Next he began to generate his own cues. Where Jacqui had emphasised one feature of a particular piece, Liam now focused on another. The pressure gauge instead of the hose. The fireman's boot instead of the wheel. And he used his own terms.

'This is the clock,' he said picking up the piece with most of the gauge on it. ' And here's another bit of clock.' He joined them.

He picked up a piece of the number-plate. 'Here's the writing. And here's some more writing.' He joined the two pieces together.

After a few more days he could complete the puzzle on his own. Mostly he worked in silence, finding pieces and putting them together in a systematic way. He didn't always work from the top down any more. He was capable of starting anywhere. He sometimes constructed the outline first, leaving a gap in the middle and completing that part last. But the talk hadn't disappeared completely. Sometimes it surfaced again, especially when he needed confirmation that what he had done was correct.

'That's the piece I was looking for,' he said on one such occasion, and he tried to put it in the puzzle. Obviously uncertain about the accuracy of what he had done, he turned to his mother. 'Is that right? Does that piece go right here?' he said, pointing at it. And Jacqui nodded in reply.

Sometimes his mother intervened if he seemed to have completely lost his way. For example, Liam would sometimes look blankly at the piece in his hand, not trying to do anything with it.

'Can you see the writing on that piece?' his mother would say. He would look at her and then back at the piece in his hand. 'Now, where's the writing on the picture?'

Liam would try the piece against a part of the number-plate already completed on the puzzle.

'That's right, ' his mother would say, and he would put it into place.

How does this incident illustrate our theoretical position on learning? We have organised our answer to this question under a series of headings to highlight key aspects of the learning process.

Principle One: learning is often a mutual accomplishment

It is important to recognise in the interactions between Liam and Jacqui the complementary nature of teaching and learning. Jacqui did her best to simplify and structure the activity of jigsaw puzzle construction for her son. At the same time Liam cooperated with his mother in an activity which he did not understand at first. He participated at his own level of understanding and his behaviour determined what Jacqui did. Barbara Rogoff (1989) explains this relationship between learning and instruction well when she writes that

> Adults do not simply solve problems and report their solutions, nor do children passively observe adults and extract the relevant information spontaneously. An adult assesses a child's current understanding of the material and adjusts the scaffolding to support the child's developing skill, while the child simultaneously adjusts the pace of instruction and guides the adult in constructing the scaffold. (p.69)

Rogoff's observation that children actively (although usually un-consciously) shape adult's contributions to any instructional session is a crucial insight into the nature of learning. Learning is collaborative, not adult-driven.

Principle Two: children often learn through guided participation

Liam had assembled puzzles before, but they had been the type that required him to place shapes in matching spaces in a board. The construction of a full picture from a set of interlocking pieces was something new. And although he had almost no idea about how to proceed, he watched and listened and took part when his mother invited him 'help' put together pieces of the puzzle. This is a clear instance of what Barbara Rogoff has called 'guided participation'. Liam learnt the purpose of the activity, as well as the manipulative skills required, by participating. At first his participation was minimal and his involvement required a great deal of guidance and support, but gradually, as his competence grew, his mother allowed him to take more and more responsibility for completion of the task.

In other words, Liam's learning depended on his being involved in the activity, from the beginning, at his current level of competence. The truly significant thing is that although his initial involvement was slight, his competence grew as his mother encouraged and allowed his involvement.

Principle Three: children profit from the support of more competent people

What is involved in these interactions between mother and child is what David Wood (1988a) refers to as the development of expertise. The expert is someone whose existing knowledge base in a specific area is both large and well organised. Expertise, Wood says

> structures the process of perception and memorisation. This makes thinking and acting fast, smooth, accurate and sensitive to error, novelty and unusual events. (p.76)

The recognition of novelty, and the ability to cope with it, is especially significant in understanding the differences between the mental functioning of adults and children. We might all find novel situations overwhelming but, as Wood points out, children are 'novices of life in general'. Like adults, children are limited in the amount of information they can deal with at one time. But they are further restricted by their limited experience of life. They are less likely to recognise a new problem as being like a similar one encountered previously. Their limited knowledge base makes it less likely that they will perceive structure and organisation in new situations. They will experience high levels of uncertainty more often than adults because they know so much less about the world. So it becomes necessary for children to enlist the assistance of someone more experienced, someone more expert. That person is often an adult who simplifies and structures the experience for them, breaking the task into more manageable sub-tasks and helping them to attend and remember; to organise and plan their activity. By so doing adults help children to overcome their limitations and make it possible for them to complete tasks which they could not manage independently.

This is what Jacqui is doing during Liam's encounter with the puzzle. She is constantly prompting Liam to attend to certain things, indeed to specific features of certain things, and she keeps reminding him of what they have done on previous occasions to complete the puzzle. She also decides how the task is to be attacked; how it is to be broken into sub-tasks that she thinks Liam will be able to manage. She is, in effect, allowing him to use her capacity to attend, her memory and her ability to choose appropriate strategies to complete the task. She is, to use a phrase from Bruner (1986), acting as 'consciousness for two'.

It is here that cognitive psychology connects with Vygotsky's work. Children who can, with assistance, complete tasks that they could not manage alone are working in what Vygotsky called a 'zone of proximal development'. The adult is helping to further develop 'ripening' functions; that is, those abilities that the child possesses but only employs when prompted to do so by a more competent other. Within this theoretical framework, adult intervention is instrumental not just in overcoming the child's immediate information overload, but in actually promoting development and shaping its direction.

There was also something far more fundamental involved in Liam's growth of expertise as a puzzle solver. As Wood (1988b) has pointed out, in order to become expert in a particular activity children have to learn what their intentions in that activity are *supposed* to be. Once Liam understood the purpose of jigsaw puzzle construction and how he could participate appropriately in the activity, he was able to engage in purposeful, independent problem solving behaviour. This is a basic feature of learning that is central to our discussion of young children engaged in learning to write.

Principle Four: effective instruction is contingent instruction

The involvement of adults who simplify and structure learning for the child does not imply direct instruction or adult control of learning. As Wood said, effective instruction involves 'leading by following'. It is essentially responsive rather than directive.

Wood's investigations of the nature of effective instruction focused on mothers instructing their four year old children in the construction of a wooden pyramid made up of several interlocking pieces. After the tutorial session the children were tested to see if they could build the pyramid independently. It was discovered that those who had learnt best were those whose mothers behaved 'contingently', in accordance with two 'rules'. The first rule specifies that failure on the part of a child to complete a sub-section of the task should cause the mother to increase her level of control. For example, if a child failed to respond to an instruction to find the big blocks, a mother following this rule would intervene more directly, perhaps by pointing to the blocks that were needed. If this brought no response, the mother might then arrange the big blocks so that the child had only to push them together to complete that section of the model. If the child still failed to respond, the mother could take her level of intervention to the final stage by actually assembling them while the child watched. In other words, the mother behaved contingently in this situation by progressively increasing her control over the act of pyramid construction.

The second rule specifies that instruction following success in completing part of the task will result in a mother providing less help or exercising less control than before. So if a mother suggests that the four big blocks should be found and the child responds by picking them up and trying to join them, the mother would withdraw and allow the child to try to complete the action independently. The mother in this situation is again behaving contingently, but now by decreasing her level of control over the construction of the model. The rules describe an inverse relationship. As the child's competence in model construction increases, the mother's level of control over the construction decreases.

One would argue that the superior pyramid builders' learning was more effective not because of the mother's teaching style but because they were just better at solving problems. To check this possibility Wood and his colleagues repeated the research study, this time matching mothers with children other than their own. Once again it was the tutor's contingency of response which seemed to be the critical factor. Children instructed by adults who behaved contingently were better at constructing the model independently.

Jacqui's tutorial behaviour, like that of the most successful mothers in Wood's research, was characterised by contingency of response. She took as much control as was necessary to keep the puzzle construction moving forward at an acceptable rate. At first Liam watched and took little part in the activity. But it was not long before he tried to do parts of it for himself. And as soon as he showed an interest in trying to take over any part of the activity, Jacqui immediately withdrew and allowed him to do so. In Bruner's (1983) observations of two mothers and their infant boys, he commented that the changes in interaction between the mothers and their children over an eighteen month period might well be summed up by: 'where there was once an observer, let there now be a participant'. This sums up Jacqui's interactions with Liam equally well. It looks as if this process of 'handover' is a fundamental aspect of learning. And it is significant that Edwards and Mercer (1987), in their study of groups of ten year olds involved in discussions with their teachers at school, also observed a transfer of control of learning from the adult to the children. It seems that it is a constant in learning across age groups.

Principle Five: it is not interaction itself but the quality of the interaction that contributes to better learning

The research cited above suggests that interaction in itself is not enough to promote successful learning. Recent research studies have investigated aspects of the relationship between social processes and learning and these provide a more detailed picture of the nature of effective tutorial interaction. For example, Barbara Rogoff and her colleagues have examined the effect of collaborative planning on learning. She concludes that children 'appear to benefit from participation in problem solving with the guidance of partners who are skilled in accomplishing the task at hand' (Rogoff, 1990, p.169). The more expert other must possess expertise which can be passed on to the novice. But social interaction, even with an expert guide, is not enough. The quality of the interaction is of crucial importance in determining the effectiveness of the learning which takes place.

In one study (Radziszewska and Rogoff, 1988) adult-child and child-child pairs were given a shopping list and a map of an imaginary downtown area with stores at which the items on the list could be purchased, and were asked to plan efficient shopping routes. Participants were later asked to complete a similar exercise independently, to establish whether they had mastered the task. In general, collaboration in adult-child pairs led to better performance on the test tasks than the collaboration in child-child pairs. But they also found that children who performed well among the adult-child groups had engaged in 'shared and guided decision making' during the first part of the study. By contrast, those who performed poorly when asked to complete the task independently had been matched with adults who used inefficient planning strategies and dominated the interaction. These partners did not talk about the strategies which might be used or involve the children in making decisions about what should be done. This was not true of Jacqui's conversations with her son. As soon as Liam had a broad understanding of the nature of the activity she began to ask him to share decisions with her (Is this the right piece? Does this one go here? etc.).

It appears, then, that children are most likely to learn effectively guided by an adult who is expert in the task being attempted, who involves them in shared decision making and discusses those decisions with them.

Principle Six: language is the means through which self-regulation of learning behaviour develops

Possibly the most significant aspect of the exchanges between Liam and Jacqui is the role language played in them. Jacqui talked constantly as she modelled jigsaw puzzle construction. She talked about what she was doing and why she was doing it. She described the pieces of puzzle in terms of the distinguishing features of each piece and how those features related to other pieces. And then when the puzzle was complete, she talked about the completed puzzle, directing Liam's attention to its elements, making him aware of it as a picture.

According to the study by Radziszewska and Rogoff, another feature of the collaboration between adults and children that seemed to contribute to effective learning was that the adults often engaged in 'strategic thinking aloud'. They not only used efficient strategies but also talked aloud about what they were doing. This is exactly what Jacqui did and Liam's rapid learning seems to testify to the effectiveness of her approach.

The role of language in learning goes beyond this, however. When Liam was able to take an active part in constructing the puzzle, and even when he could complete it independently, language remained an integral part of the activity. First he used his mother's talk as a model which he used to guide him in his completion of the task. As Vygotsky (1978, p.28) has said, the talk shaped the activity into a structure just as a mould gives shape to a substance. The conversations with his mother continued to guide him. He used her words and phrases to focus his attention on the features of the puzzle which were relevant at each point in its completion and to cue his memory of what was to be done and in what order. Liam had learnt to use the dialogue with his mother to regulate his own behaviour.

It did not stop there. He then began to generate his own words and phrases, exercising conscious control over what he was doing, and even sometimes providing a metacommentary on his actions (e.g. 'That's not the piece I'm looking for. This is.'). And even when he had mastered the puzzle, working quickly and quietly on his own, language still surfaced at times. But the direction clearly seems to have been from the control of his behaviour by his mother, to overt self-direction and finally to internalised self-direction. We cannot be absolutely sure that covert language did exercise control over his behaviour as he worked quietly on the puzzle, but the general direction of his use of language as he learnt the puzzle certainly seems to suggest that this is what happened.

Principle Seven: learning depends upon the negotiation of meaning

Imagine a child being asked to describe one of a series of six drawings of a man so that a listener could identify it. Each man holds either a small balloon or a large balloon which is either red, green or blue. Each drawing can be identified by a statement discriminating it from all other possible choices (e.g. 'Point to the man holding the small red balloon'). It has been found that children under seven are likely to provide ambiguous messages for a listener (e.g. The man has a green balloon). Similar results have been found when children are asked to listen to messages instead of giving them. Children under seven are likely to react to an ambiguous message like 'Show me the man with the green balloon' by choosing one of the two possible choices instead of seeking clarification by asking a question ('a big balloon or a small one?'). These studies reveal aspects of the difficulties young children are thought to have with referential communication; that is, the ability to produce clear spoken messages and to recognise when heard messages are not clear (Robinson, Goelman and Olson, 1983; Robinson and Robinson, 1985; Robinson and Whittaker, 1986; Robinson and Whittaker, 1987).

Peter Lloyd has brought a sociolinguistic perspective to the study of referential communication (1991, 1992, 1993). To understand referential communication, he says, the reciprocal nature of conversation must be considered. Success or failure in communication is seen from this perspective to depend on the negotiation of understanding through conversation, especially the asking of questions designed to bring responses which will clarify, confirm or elaborate on information previously received. Lloyd found that while younger children were much more likely to produce inadequate messages, they were also much less likely to respond to an inadequate message with a request for further information. In other words they are much less likely to engage in a negotiation of meaning with their conversational partner.

Lloyd (1990) also speculates about why young children apparently find it difficult to detect and deal with ambiguity. In everyday life, he says, adults respond to children's feedback, providing support for them when they seem puzzled or uncertain. The familiar adult is not just a resource from whom young children can obtain needed information, ' ... but also an extension of the child's cognitive and communicative system – a communicative support system'(pp.64-69). Lloyd argues that in normal situations adults make dialogue with young children possible by performing a number of communicative functions. These functions include focusing the child's attention on what is relevant; simplifying and interpreting information for the child; holding information in working memory for the child's use; reminding the child of what is known and what the goal of the dialogue is; alerting the child to communicative success and failure; and shifting the child to an alternative procedure when the present one is failing. He suggests that when this 'communicative support system' fails to function in the usual way, children start to behave in an aberrant manner. They might, for example, stop asking questions and agree with whatever the adult suggests, as they often do in the experimental situation. It is not, therefore, the behaviour of children which is strange in such situations but the behaviour of adults.

Jacqui provides Liam with communicative support. As a result, although he is only three, he does ask clarifying questions of his mother. He asks, 'Does this piece go here?' and 'Is that right?', looking at his mother for confirmation. He is capable of jointly constructing meaning with his mother in the pursuit of a mutual goal. His mother responds to the clues he gives (which are often non-verbal) indicating uncertainty and confusion, and she guides him and 'fills in' for him to ensure that their interaction can continue. This certainly supports the claim that, in natural situations, children are capable of quite sophisticated negotiation of meaning through language at an early stage of their development, albeit with people with whom they share a common background of experience and close emotional ties and whose primary aim, when they talk with their children, is to sustain the dialogue by whatever means.

Competence in referential communication would seem to be essential to children if they are to learn with, and from, other people. At school, children need to be able to determine the teacher's referential intent in order to learn. Yet, as we have said above, the research evidence suggests that young children have difficulty in recognising when they do not understand and in seeking information to clear up confusions in communication. The fact that Liam seemed able to seek confirmation through questioning at a much earlier age than research findings indicate, suggests that children might go to school far better able to negotiate meanings than has previously been thought. Perhaps teachers should give more attention to creating circumstances which make it easier for children to ask questions and resolve misunderstandings. Certainly the excellent teachers we have worked with do this without conscious effort. They get to know their children very well, they build a background of shared experience which forms a basis for talk, and they allow children to use the linguistic competence they bring to school with them (including their knowledge of how to use language to get things done). In their classrooms the negotiation of meanings is visible to those who trouble to look, and learning proceeds smoothly because the focus is on the construction of meaning and the maintenance of communication.

Conclusion

We have gone to some lengths to make our assumptions and beliefs about learning clear. Put in the simplest possible way, we have positioned ourselves with those who believe that learning is social and collaborative in nature. This is not to say that children learn only through social interaction. But it does mean that learning can only be adequately understood if its social nature is taken into account. Learning is social both in what is learnt (for example, writing is a valued social achievement) and in the learning process (that is, the dialogue which facilitates learning and eventually becomes the basis for thought itself). This position is basically Vygotskian and Barbara Rogoff sums it up when she says that '...individual development of higher mental processes cannot be understood without considering the social roots of both the tools for thinking that children are learning to use and the social interactions that guide children in their use' (Rogoff, 1990, p.35).

The most casual observations reveal that when children have trouble in learning something, they naturally turn to more competent others to help them through their difficulties. And our prolonged observations of children learning to read and write have convinced us that they very often achieve far more with assistance than they could have managed alone. This raises a crucial question: how important is adult intervention in children's learning? It should be clear from what we have said that we believe children can benefit from the assistance of adults when they are learning. Social interaction facilitates understanding and promotes development, and it helps children to relate what they have learnt independently to what is known by people generally. But is teaching a prequisite for learning, as Beard and Oakhill suggest? And if this is not the case, then what exactly is the role of instruction in learning?

In any discussion about the nature of the relationship between instruction and learning we need to recognise that learning is primary. Different sets of assumptions about learning will necessarily produce different approaches to instruction. In a recent publication Rogoff, Matusov and White (1996) identify three models of instruction based on specific positions on learning. First is the 'adult-run' model which corresponds with '... theoretical notions that learning is a process managed by experts who transmit knowledge to learners'. Second is the 'children-run' model of instruction which corresponds with '... theoretical notions that learning is the province of learners who acquire knowledge through their active exploration'. The third is a 'community of learners' model which corresponds with '... the theoretical stance that learning involves transformation of participation in collaborative endeavour'. The models differ essentially in where the responsibility for promoting learning is placed. The first two positions are one-sided. In adult-run instruction the teacher manages the learning activities and is seen to be centrally responsible for promoting learning in the child. In children-run instruction children choose their own activities while the adult's main responsibility is to provide an enriched and stimulating learning environment. By contrast the community of learners model involves mutuality of responsibility despite '... some asymmetries in roles and responsibilities'.

It seems to us that the position put by Beard and Oakhill is an expression of an 'adult-run' model of instruction. And that their critique of *Read With Me* is a reaction to what they perceive as Liz Waterland's 'children-run' model of instruction. Recognising this places the debate about reading instruction in a broader framework. It focuses attention on the fact that debates about competing approaches to literacy instruction are really concerned with the different views of learning upon which the approaches are based. Our own position on learning implies an approach to instruction much like that which is embodied in a 'community of learners' model. In a classroom operating in accordance with this model, responsibility for learning is shared. Adults and children will be collaboratively engaged in learning activities, with the adults often guiding and supporting the children's learning. Amongst other things, the children learn to participate in the management of their own learning. Everyone works together, with everyone being a resource for everyone else (Rogoff, Matusov and White, 1996).

This book attempts to show that such a model can be successfully applied to literacy learning in the context of ordinary classrooms. We maintain that the 'one-adult-to-many children' ratio that exists in most classrooms need not prevent learning from proceeding as a social and collaborative activity. In the next four chapters we describe and analyse what happened over the period of a full school year in a class of five-year-olds as they learnt to write. Like the mothers in the studies conducted by Wood and Bruner, the teacher of this class structured and simplified the instructional context to make learning easier for the children. She provided support which helped the children to remember and attend and plan more effectively. She responded contingently by providing assistance when it was needed but then withdrawing and handing over control whenever the children showed themselves capable of proceeding independently. She constantly encouraged them to seek solutions to their own problems and to use the other children in the class as a resource for learning.

At the same time the children, like those in Rogoff's studies, learned by becoming involved in shared thinking and joint decision-making with their teacher. They learned to regulate their mental processes through social interaction with her. They negotiated meanings and solved problems both by themselves and with the assistance of others. At the beginning of the year the teacher needed to give them high levels of support to maintain their participation in the writing sessions in the classroom. But by the end of the year they were participating independently in literacy activities, learning about writing not just when they were involved in dialogue with their teacher but also when they were doing such things as reading books, discussing their writing with other children and listening in to conversations between other members of the class.

The learning we observed going on in this classroom is appropriately described, in Rogoff's terms, as a transformation of participation (Rogoff, Matusov and White, 1996; Rogoff and Toma, 1997). As the year progressed the children learned to participate more effectively in the literacy activities and gradually assumed more responsibility for learning. At the same time the adults also went through a transformation of participation, passing control to the children as they seem ready to accept it, and supporting and guiding the children's thinking rather than prompting and organising it. The instructional model is neither adult-run nor children-run, but involves truly collaborative acts of learning.

The type of instructional model which functions in any classroom is also important for another reason. It tells the children what types of learners the teacher considers them to be. This means that the teacher who insists that children must be taught in order to learn is telling the children that they are dependent on instruction. On the other hand, the teacher who involves the children in collaborative thinking and hands control to them as they are able to accept it, tells the children that they are capable of incidental learning and independent problem solving. That is why the five-year-olds we observed became confident and independent writers during their first year of formal schooling.

We are claiming that learning which is social and collaborative will not only lead to more efficient learning but will also produce better learners. We have cited a number of psychological studies in support of this position but it is our experience in classrooms over many years which has really been the primary influence on what we believe. We have cited psychological research, but we are not psychologists. Nor are we sociolinguists or anthropologists. We are educators. We began our working lives as teachers of primary age children and as we became researchers, the questions we asked and the answers we formed were still related to our personal experience of teaching children to read and write. That is why we insisted on looking at children learning in classrooms and why we are unconvinced by accounts of literacy development based on the information processing models of human cognition. Our observations of children in their own classrooms have convinced us that it is only possible to understand how children become literate if we study them in natural and familiar settings like the school and home. If the children we studied had been taken away from the environment and people they knew and had been prevented from gaining access to the resources they routinely used for writing, we could not have gained any accurate or reliable impressions of what had contributed to their growth in competence as readers and writers. Neither would we have been able to understand the process by which they became literate if we had not observed and recorded the changes that occurred over a significant period of time. What was learnt in any one session was not always immediately obvious. Often it was only with the passage of time, after children had been given repeated opportunities to test thier hypotheses about written language, that development in their competence became clear.

Each chapter, therefore, deals in detail with children learning in natural settings. In Chapters Two to Six we describe and explain how two five-year-olds learned to write in their first year of school. On the basis of this analysis we make suggestions about the nature of literacy learning and the role played by adults in helping children to learn. In Chapter Seven we describe the patterns of instruction in a fourth grade classroom and we examine in detail an exchange between the teacher and a nine-year-old girl who had just transferred into the class from another school, bringing with her a belief that she was dependent on instruction. We describe what the teacher did to try to alter the child's approach to learning and indicate that the patterns of collaborative talk, through which learning is achieved, are essentially the same as they were in the class of five-year-olds. In Chapter Eight we describe how a teacher of developmentally delayed children built her literacy programme on the belief that her children, like all other children, would learn more efficiently if the learning they did was social and collaborative. What happened in that classroom suggests that learning is of the same nature for all children regardless of age or ability. Finally, in Chapter Nine, we examine what a gifted eleven-year-old writer had to tell us about the way she learnt to read and write. Through an analysis of interviews with her and her parents we consider what learning to be literate should involve, not just for the gifted but for all children.

With the exception of the child in Chapter Six, this book is about successful learners, because we believe that we can learn most from such children. Understanding how effective learners gain control over reading and writing can, we believe, guide teachers in the development and delivery of better literacy programmes. In the next chapter, therefore, we will start to explain how the children and adults whom we observed and interviewed worked together, both at home and at school, not only on learning to be literate, but also on becoming independent, flexible and confident learners and thinkers.

Chapter 2

Emma is five years and eight months old and she has been at school since early February. It is now October. She could not read or write when she came to school but she is now confidently writing stories during the regular writing sessions in her kindergarten classroom in a New South Wales school. She still needs assistance at times but she usually writes texts consisting of three to six sentences during these sessions. Her teacher is Rhonda Fisher.

Charles, who is sitting next to Emma, is writing a story which he has titled The Ghost. Emma is writing about a fish. She writes ' Once upon a time there was a fish' without any assistance. She writes 'She livb'. Rhonda notices what Emma has written so she asks one of the other children, Damien, to help. With his assistance Emma corrects her spelling of the word.

Then Rhonda asks, 'Where did your fish live?'

Emma: in a pool

She makes eye contact with Rhonda.

Rhonda: what kind of pool?

Charles: a muddy pool?

Emma looks at him and smiles.

Charles: *a shallow pool?*

Rhonda: *was it a * was it a*

Emma: a *blue* pool

Rhonda: in a blue * *was it a pool* like where the nice frogs lived?

27

The Fizh

Once upon a Time There woz a Fizn
She livd ino Blackpool oll by her self,
And She woz very ow becouse She woz
ciCRAd evey day She Crid And iCrid
becouze She dad no children
But Then! She dad a pop
She dad a new boot. Then She
woz so hope.

Emma's complete text: 17th October

Charles: *was it a shallow one?*

Emma is still maintaining eye contact with Rhonda. She nods and then prepares to write.

Charles: was it a shallow or a deep pool

Emma makes eye contact with Charles.

Charles: a shallow or a deep pool?

Emma: deep

She writes 'in'.

Rhonda: a deep blue pool is it?

Emma: yes

Emma writes 'in a'.

She writes 'blo' for 'blue' by segmenting it into sounds and matching sounds with letters. She writes 'pool' as she says it. When Rhonda notices how Emma has spelled 'blue' she draws her attention to the Do You Know Your Colours chart and Emma adds 'ue' to the end of 'blo'. Rhonda does not pursue this further. Emma writes 'all by her' and then stops. She seems unable to manage to segment 'self' into its constituent sounds although she can do this with many words. Rhonda eventually intervenes and does the phonemic segmentation for her. Emma writes letters to match the sounds as Rhonda says them. The text at this point in the writing session is:

once upon a Time There was a Fish

She lived in a bloue pool all by her Self.

Rhonda now looks down at Emma's story and reads from it.

Rhonda: she lived in a blue pool all by herself

Emma looks down as Rhonda says 'lived' and starts to read along with her.

Emma: blue pool all by herself

Rhonda: so what's going to happen to her?

Emma looks down and shapes to write. Then she looks up again and makes eye contact with Rhonda.

Rhonda:	remember how I said if once you finished one idea and then you wanted to start another idea what could you put?
Emma:	a full stop
Rhonda:	and you can start another sentence then can't you because
Emma:	not another story
Rhonda:	no no not another story but another sentence because really a story is a lot of sentences
Emma:	you don't have to say 'and'
Rhonda:	that's right * you don't have to say 'and' all the time so you can put a full stop and then you can start * (Emma puts a full stop after 'herself') that's right
Rhonda:	what * after you put a full stop what do you have to put in then?
Damien:	a capital letter
Rhonda:	yes (she nods at Damien).

Emma looks down at her story.

Emma:	she lived in a * a

She stops to listen to the talk going on between Rhonda and some of the other children about how to write a word. Then she starts to read her own text again, pointing as she reads.

Emma:	in a ** blue pool at * all by herself.

Several things are happening during this exchange. Emma is using phonemic segmentation to spell unknown words but Rhonda obviously thinks that she is sufficiently advanced in her writing development to profit from having her attention drawn to conventional ways of spelling. On the other hand, when Emma does not correct 'blue' properly Rhonda does not persist. Emma has had her attention drawn to the relevant source of information and Rhonda seems to be content with that for the moment. Other matters are more important.

For example, when she asks Emma what is going to happen to her fish she is passing to the child the responsibility for making decisions about a significant aspect of her writing. Emma is beginning to learn about the omniscience and omnipotence that authors of fiction enjoy. She is being drawn into experiences that will eventually lead her to understand what Kurt Vonnegut Junior tells one of his characters in *Breakfast of Champions*. Vonnegut has intruded himself into his novel. He has been following his chief character, Kilgore Trout, down a darkened street in his car. Trout is trying to escape from him but has now stopped running and stands looking apprehensively at the person talking to him from the darkened interior of the car. Vonnegut tells Trout not to be afraid. ' I am a novelist,' he says. 'I created you for use in one of my books. Are there any questions you'd like to ask?'

Trout is not comforted. 'Do you have a gun?' he asks.

'I don't need a gun to control you, Mr. Trout,' Vonnegut replies 'All I have to do is write something down and that's it.'

Emma is learning that she has that same power. It's the greatest gift written language offers; the capacity to create possible worlds which can be manipulated in endless ways to explore ideas and test hypotheses.

We are not saying that Emma has reached this sophisticated level of written language use at this point in her development as a writer, only that within the first few months of entering school as a non-writer, Emma is already beginning to make decisions about what's going to happen next in her story. She is already learning that all she has to do is write something down and that's it. She can create any world she wants.

And it isn't just the teacher who is involved in this instructional conversation. Charles also engages Emma in a discussion about the details of her imagined world. Is it a muddy pool or a clear one? Is it deep or shallow? Rhonda joins in again. 'Was it a pool like where the nice frogs lived?' Implicitly Rhonda is drawing Emma's attention to the fact that what has been read in story books can become a source of ideas for what might be written. And there is something else going on too. Emma is also talking to Rhonda about writing itself. About where to insert full stops; about the difference between sentences and stories; and about matters of style and sentence structure (you don't have to say 'and').

There is still an enormous amount for Emma to learn about writing. But she has come a long way in a short time and we should not lose sight of this in the discussions of Rhonda's classroom that follow. In the months between February and October Emma and most of her classmates developed an impressive control of writing as an activity and they also began to develop some sense of the power of literacy as a tool of thought. In this chapter, and the three that follow it, we will describe in detail how that happened.

Talking and Learning in Rhonda's Classroom

Children learn more quickly in some classrooms than in others and it seems obvious that the attention of researchers should be focused on classrooms where learning seems to occur with little effort. We can learn most about efficient learning from observing efficient learners. We can learn most about effective instruction by watching effective instructors. So it is enlightening to examine closely what happened in Rhonda Fisher's classroom so that we might understand what made it possible for the children she taught to learn so rapidly.

Next we provide a broad description of the regular literacy activities of Rhonda's classroom. Two things need to be kept in mind as it is read. First, the different activities were complementary in nature. While our descriptions might sometimes make these activities sound as if each were a separate and independent part of the literacy programme, they really constitute a cohesive group of experiences. Memories of any one activity were routinely drawn upon during the other activities to support and inform the learning that was going on. Second, the activities described do not include the incidental conversations about literacy that occurred constantly in this classroom. Throughout the school day Rhonda spoke briefly to various children about what they were reading and writing. Even during the sessions we recorded, when she was concentrating her attention on one of the children we had selected for observation, other children came seeking her assistance. These were brief exchanges, but during them Rhonda responded to each child differently in terms of what she already knew about that child's knowledge and competence as a writer. In fact, it was Rhonda's knowledge of the children as individuals which was the critical factor in solving each problem and thus promoting learning. Being aware of what they knew, and remembering what they had done recently, Rhonda was able to help the children solve their problems by referring to relevant shared knowledge and experience which might otherwise have been overlooked.

Remembering what each child in a class of thirty knows and can do might seem to make extraordinary demands on a teacher's memory but, as Roger Brown (1980) has pointed out, it is no more than we do in everyday life. We keep 'running accounts' on a number of friends, colleagues at work, remote relatives and so on. We remember many things about them, including '... what things one has shared with each, disclosed to each, and dissembled with each' (p.202). But we only remember such things because we interact with these people individually in mutually intelligible conversations in familiar settings. The teacher's knowledge of the children in his or her class has the same basis. If the only activities in a classroom are teacher-directed lessons and closely supervised set work which is evaluated in terms of preconceived standards of correctness, teachers will learn little about the children in their care. But if many opportunities exist for teachers to talk individually with the children in their classes they will soon develop what Brown calls an 'apperceptive mass' of knowledge about each child which can be tapped at appropriate times to assist in decision-making, problem-solving and even just making sense of casual conversational exchanges. The importance of this aspect of learning cannot be over-emphasised.

None of the literacy activities described below is new but they need to be outlined to provide a context for the discussions in the following chapters. If there is anything new it is that they form a cohesive, complementary group of experiences which is drawn upon by the teacher or the children every time writing is used in the classroom. They are the source of the collective memory of the class, aspects of which are continually brought to mind in order to solve immediate problems and develop understandings which will make it possible for the children to further develop their competence as writers.

• Reading and talking about classroom print

There was print everywhere in Rhonda's classroom. Signs on the door (This is the door); on Rhonda's desk (Mrs. Fisher sits here); displays of days of the week and months of the year; alphabet charts; numbers;

words on the chalkboard; poetry charts on the wall and so on. As the year went on, copies of the children's written texts were displayed on the classroom walls. Charts of frequently used words appeared. Word cards in the large folder at the front of the room grew in number. And more and more books were read to the children and left in accessible places in the classroom.

More was needed than just the presence of the printed words in the classroom to make them part of the taken-for-granted knowledge shared by the teacher and the children. Rhonda had to make the children aware of the written language in the classroom by regularly reading it with them. She also involved the children in searching for words. This was a shared, highly structured activity. At the early stages what was to be remembered was where the word might be found, not the word itself. For example, Rhonda might ask, 'Where can we find the word 'piano'?' She would then establish joint attention on the various written signs in the room, reading each one with the children in turn until they came to 'This is the piano'. Having found the right display of print the next step was to distinguish the needed word from the others on the sign or chart. So Rhonda would read it again, pointing to each word as it was read. 'This is the piano. All right. This word (putting her finger on it) says piano. What letter does it start with? Come out and read the sign for me Amy. Point to the words as you say them. Charles come and show me which word says piano.' And so on.

Later, if children wanted to use the word 'piano' they would not just be told how to spell the word but would be reminded of the shared experience of having found it during the familiar word search sessions. The functional nature of the classroom print would also help them. 'Piano' is likely to be one of the words on the sign attached to that musical instrument, not to the door or the teacher's table. And, because they would have had many experiences of locating the precise word needed in a display, they would know that they should 'read' the print, word by word, left to right, until the needed one was identified. At this stage in the children's writing development what is involved in knowing how to write words, is not the simple recall of how a particular word is spelled, but a familiarity with the available print, an awareness of its functional nature, and a capacity to recall and employ the structure of the 'word search' activity.

• Learning words

At the beginning of the year Rhonda taught her students a set of words using *Breakthrough to Literacy* materials (Mackay, Thompson and Schaub, 1970). The children did not keep individual Sentence Makers with words in them. Instead, but there was a large Sentence Maker at the front of the room and as each word was introduced to the children the appropriate card was put into the folder. In the first few weeks Rhonda introduced a new word each day, so more than twenty words were soon on display. The fact that Rhonda had introduced each of these words to the class by constructing sentences including them and then asking the children to copy the sentence or complete a worksheet, did not mean that they could then be recalled at will. This basic group of words simply formed part of the body of print on display in the classroom. Rhonda not only made the words learnt in this way the objects of word search activities but also included them in her blackboard stories. And when she spoke to the children about their writing, either in groups or individually, she would frequently remind them about known words on display in the large Sentence Maker or on charts of frequently used words attached to the walls of the classroom. Once again what seemed to be important at the early stages was not whether a specific word could be instantly recalled but whether the circumstances of its being taught, and its location amongst the other print in the classroom, could be remembered. Since the children were being asked to 'write a story' each day, Rhonda was trying to build up a group of familiar words as quickly as possible so that they might be more confident about trying to write a meaningful text rather than writing strings of letters, lists of known words or just drawing a picture.

• Reading and talking about Big Books

Big Books are large format books which can be seen by everyone in the class at the same time. During repeated readings of these books Rhonda drew the children's attention to such things as frequently repeated words, grapho-phonemic relationships in words, words which were similar in form to each other, print conventions and so on. In one session we recorded, about four weeks into the first term of the school year, Rhonda used a story called *The Magic Fish*. She had already read it to the class a number of times.

She first put the book on display and then asked the children to tell her what the story was called. Then she asked nominated children to identify 'fish' in the title. Next she said, ' What's on the end of fish? Someone asked me about 'sh' yesterday. Fish. Who can tell what part of 'fish' says 'sh'?' Most of the children seemed to know.

Then she turned to the first page. 'How does it start?' she asked. 'A lot of stories start like this.' One child volunteered 'Once upon a time.' Rhonda smiled. 'That's right. Once upon a time.' She started to read the story and pointed to the words as she said them. The first sentence contained the word 'fisherman'. Rhonda covered 'fisher'. 'What does this say?' she asked. Several children said 'man'. It is a word that Rhonda has taught them to recognise.

There would seem to be two main purposes to these sessions. One is to focus the children's attention on the features of the text which might otherwise go unnoticed: to make them conscious of specific features of written language so that they know how to look at printed language. The second is to establish points of reference in the shared memory of the group which could be recalled at appropriate moments. 'Remember when we read *The Magic Fish*. Who can remember what the word 'fish' ends with?' Or 'We saw 'ghost' when we were reading *The Haunted House*. I said there was something special about the word ghost. Who can remember what it was?'

• Finding something to write about

One of the great problems children had at first was being able to frame a 'story' in preparation for the writing session. When the children finally understood how to choose a suitable topic for writing and were able to frame a statement about it in language appropriate to the production of a written text, a breakthrough point seemed to be reached. At least two things seemed to be involved in learning to do this. The first was developing an understanding of the potential uses of writing (e.g. to record and reflect upon personal experience). The second was developing an awareness of the decontextualised nature of written language. Written texts had to provide their own context in order to be intelligible to readers.

To help the children to learn about choosing topics and framing written language messages, Rhonda found it necessary, for about the first three months, to construct a 'story' jointly with each child before they were sent back to their desks to write. A typical session during the first month of the school year ran something like this.

Rhonda asks the class. 'Who's got a good story today?' Some children put their hands up.

Rhonda asks Stephanie, 'Well, what are you going to write about?'

Stephanie says, 'My birthday party.'

'When is it going to be?'

'On Saturday.'

'Well you could write that,' Rhonda says. "My birthday party is on Saturday'. What's the first word?'

Jonathon tells her that he doesn't know what he is going to write.

'Aren't you doing something exciting at the weekend? What are you doing on Saturday?'

'We're going camping.'

'Well you can write that. 'We're going camping' What's the first word?'

She asks Stirling what he is going to write.

'Mrs Fisher sits here,' he says.

'All right .' says Rhonda, ' Where can you see that. Point to it.'

He points to the sign attached to the teacher's desk.

Another child says, 'I'm going to draw a picture.'

Rhonda says, 'All right.'

Clare says, 'Riding on my bike.'

'Well you could write 'I can ride on my bike".

Rhonda has written 'bike' on the chalkboard earlier.

'Where could you find 'bike'? Amy, help her.'

Amy points to the word on the chalkboard.

Rhonda responds to each child in terms of what she knows they might reasonably be expected to attempt. With some she insists on the construction of a coherent story and she helps them to get started. With others she is content if they nominate something purposeful to do.

When they return to their desks not even those who have constructed a suitable story with Rhonda's assistance necessarily attempt to write anything. Instead of writing the agreed upon 'story' they might draw pictures or copy words. It does not matter at first that they don't write. It is the routine as a whole that is being made familiar: first the blackboard story; then working out their own story and then the writing session. Not much is needed to start taking part. They participate at whatever level they can. That is the important thing, because it is through participation that they learn about the purpose of the activity and develop their understanding of its structure. Eventually, as Rhonda persists in helping them to frame stories, and as they become familiar with more words and the blackboard stories give them both ideas for topics and ways of writing words, they make their first attempts at writing a text of their own.

By the middle of the year these preparatory sessions were no longer needed. Topic choice and framing a 'story' were no longer any trouble. These matters became part of the assumed basis upon which the writing sessions proceeded, and other things became the focus of attention and the subject of talk between the teacher and the children and among the children themselves. Later we discuss in more detail what happened at that stage of development.

• Taking part in joint story constructions

It was primarily through their involvement in the 'blackboard story' sessions, which Rhonda conducted three times a week, that the children learnt how to participate in the activity of 'writing a story' as it was practised in her classroom. These sessions also drew upon what was learnt in other literacy activities and even incorporated some of them into its structure. For example, the things that were learnt about words in the Big Book sessions were used in constructing the group stories: apostrophes, spelling generalisations, the uses of capital letters and so on. And the routine of searching for words became a sub-routine within the overall structure of 'story writing'.

These blackboard stories served many purposes but here are some of the most important:

1. Learning to listen to speech

David Olson (1996) has challenged the widely held belief that writing is the transcription of speech. Instead, he says, writing provides a conceptual model for speech. The models of language provided by our scripts, he continues

> ...are both what is acquired in the process of learning to read and write and what is employed in thinking about language; writing is in principle metalinguistics. ... Writing systems create the categories in terms of which we become conscious of speech. (p.89)

What we observed in Rhonda Fisher's classroom showed this happening. Through their involvement in the construction of 'blackboard stories' the children learned to listen to speech as if it was made up of constituent sounds that could be represented by letters of the alphabet.

2. Recognising the activity type

John Gumperz (1982) has defined a contextualisation cue as '...any feature of linguistic form that contributes to the signalling of contextual presupposition'. In other words, it is something that speakers use to signal to listeners what is to be taken-for-granted and what is to be foregrounded in the particular activity type which is about to begin. Any utterance, Gumperz says, can be understood in any number of ways. In practice, people make decisions about how to interpret what is being said, based on their definition of what is happening at the time of interaction. They make these judgements in relation to communicative frames which are 'identifiable and familiar'. That is, in order to participate appropriately in a given type of activity they must recognise what type of activity it is, what the normal patterns of interaction are, and what constitutes acceptable behaviour within the boundaries of such an activity. We know a young man who was pulled over by a police car for speeding. When the highway patrolman asked him if he had seen the speed restriction signs he said, 'No. I was going too fast.' He was speaking as one young man might to another in a friendly conversation. He had misread the contextualisation cues. The policeman interpreted the remark not as a friendly overture but as insolence. The exchange did not go well for our young friend.

In Rhonda's classroom it was mainly through participation in the black-board story sessions that the children learnt to recognise 'story writing' as a highly patterned activity. They learnt quickly that when Rhonda said something like, 'All right. Listen to my story today,' they were about to be involved in 'writing a story'. Her positioning at the black-board with a stick of chalk in her hand gave further indications that she was intending not only to tell them what her story was but was also going to write it on the chalkboard. Only when they were able to recog-nise the 'story writing' activity type were they able to interpret reliably the speech and action of the people taking part in the activity with them.

3. Learning the activity structure

This activity draws everything together. The children have to know what steps they need to go through in order to write a story success-fully. During the construction of the story Rhonda enticed and coerced the children into joint decision-making. She also engaged in 'strategic thinking aloud' (Rogoff, 1991). She did not just construct the story – she talked about how it was being constructed; about what she was thinking and the decisions she was making. These steps in Rhonda's writing activity structure are roughly as follows:

i)   Making a clear statement about what is going to be written.
ii)   Identifying each word in succession.
iii)   Either
       a.   recalling the identified word from memory
       b.   finding it in the print environment of the classroom and copying it
       c.   segmenting it into phonemes and making sound-symbol matches.
iv)   Re-reading the developing text in order to remember what has already been written and what remains to be written.

Knowledge of the activity structure is a prerequisite to developing competence as a writer. Having it under control does not make the child a writer but until they can use it they have little chance of developing as writers.

4. Making the task manageable

If the children are to complete a task like 'writing a story' independently, they have to know how to break it into a series of more manageable sub-tasks. This is a large part of what is learnt in learning the activity structure, but it needs to be emphasised because it is such an important part of learning to think about writing (and most other things). At first the adult does the work of dividing the task into more manageable sub-units. Eventually the children do it for themselves.

5. Learning how to look at words

The 'blackboard story' sessions were also concerned with showing the children how to attend to important details in words. For example, during these sessions Rhonda usually accepted invented spellings, but after the story had been completed she would write a conventionally spelled version of the text directly underneath and ask the children to compare the invented spellings with the conventionally spelled words. By this means critical differences in words became the focus of attention. Word searches similarly required the children to attend to displays of words and distinguish the target word from others on the same chart or sign. And in reading the Big Books, Rhonda drew attention not only to words that were similar in form but also to specific identifying features of words like the 'h' in 'ghost' and the apostrophe in 'we're'.

• Developing awareness of book language

Rhonda read to the children frequently. Some stories were favourites and were read often. One such story was *The Gingerbread Man*. When the story was thoroughly known she said to the children, 'We're not going to read the story today. We're going to see if we can tell it. If it's not a true story, how does it start?'

> Several children offered, 'once upon a time', and then, 'once upon a time there was a little old lady and a little old man.'
>
> Rhonda asks, 'Well, what happened?'
>
> The story was pieced together. Rhonda kept checking the accuracy of what was said, trying to prompt accurate recall of the text. 'Is that what happens in the book?' she kept asking.
>
> Then she allocated roles and helped the children to dramatise the story, insisting that the language of the book was reproduced as closely as possible. The children corrected each other if events were out of sequence.

At the appropriate moments Rhonda invited group participation. 'Let's help the gingerbread man say that,' she said. And they all joined in, 'You can run and run as fast as you can but you won't catch me, I'm the gingerbread man.'

'Do we need the book to remember the story?' Rhonda asked.

'No,' they chorused.

This is just one more way to make language itself the topic of discussion. The story had to be deliberately thought about in order to reproduce it. Its precise use of language became the focus of attention. Through their involvement in such activities, the children were being made aware of the special nature of written language. Later some of them tried to re-tell the story in writing. 'Once upon a time' became a commonly used story beginning. And as the children wrote their own stories they started to refer to class copies of *The Gingerbread Man* to find out how to spell 'once upon a time' and other words they needed.

• Writing stories

All the children were involved from the first week in individual 'writing sessions', although not even the most advanced were able to write more than a few words at first. It was, nevertheless, important that these sessions were part of the programme because it was as Rhonda helped the children to write simple sentences that she discovered what they could do with her assistance. In other words, it was during these sessions that she established their zones of proximal development, discovering what their 'ripening functions' were so that she could help bring them to maturity. Being able to write with assistance today was indeed a predictor of what they would be able to do independently in the very near future.

The children naturally set their own rate of progress. Rhonda provided interesting experiences and then used those experiences as the topics for jointly constructed stories. She also wrote about familiar things – what was done at school, for example. This helped the children to find safe, manageable topics and to be confident that they would be able to write most of the words that the topic required. So they wrote texts like: 'Yesterday we had our Pet Show'; 'Today we are going to walk up Mount Keira'; and 'At school we write stories and our mums come to hear us read'.

While this might seem to be limiting it turned out not to be so. While beginnings of stories might be standard, the children usually built in accounts of personal experience and comments on what had happened. And the routine stories inevitably led on to genuinely personal and individual writing. This did not happen every day but the writing of safe, manageable texts built confidence and competence so that when the need to write something personal arose, the children were equal to the task.

Conclusion

Edwards and Mercer (1987) say that a society's educational system has its own epistemological culture, and that an important function of education is the 'cognitive socialisation' of the children. Teachers, they say,

> ... have the task of 'scaffolding' children's first steps towards and into this culture, of supervising their entry into the universe of educational discourse. This is done by creating, through joint action and talk with the child, a contextual framework for educational activities. (p.161)

The children in Rhonda's class had to learn how to behave as literate members of their culture. In the first instance, that meant learning to behave like readers and writers within the more restricted culture of their own classroom. To help them to do this Rhonda first had to establish a contextual framework for this type of educational activity. Context, as Edwards and Mercer define it, is the common knowledge shared by the participants which is invoked by the discourse. Establishing a context, then, meant invoking those physical aspects of the environment and those shared experiences which would permit the children to behave as writers. For example, the words on a chart in the room became contextual when Rhonda referred to them. The morning's blackboard story became contextual when Rhonda reminded the children about it. A book that had been shared became contextual when Rhonda mentioned it. And Rhonda had to ensure that the structure of the story writing activity remained contextual by constantly reminding the children about the series of steps which had to be taken in order to produce an acceptable written language text.

In time, Rhonda no longer needed to invoke certain things as contextual. The children became familiar with the steps involved in writing a story. They referred spontaneously to charts and books as sources of information about how to write the words they needed. In other words, certain things became part of the taken-for-granted, shared knowledge which made it possible for the children to negotiate new understandings of writing. And so new areas of common knowledge were established which formed the basis for yet further growth in understanding and competence. And so it went.

Edwards and Mercer say that the '...extent to which educational knowledge is made 'common' through classroom discourse is one measure of the effectiveness of the educational process'. This is what we try to trace for the reader. We attempt to show that as the things that were contextual at the beginning became presupposed knowledge – new aspects of the writing process were foregrounded so that they could be attended to and thought about by the children. Because these changes in the development of common knowledge are often clearly evident in the data we collected, we are able to explain clearly the processes involved in becoming a writer in Rhonda's classroom. In this chapter we have explained how Rhonda 'scaffolded' the children's first steps into the culture of writing. We go on to explain in detail what happened as the children's writing competence developed during the school year.

Chapter 3

The next three chapters concentrate on two girls from Rhonda's kindergarten class: Emma and Hannelore. It is early February in the middle of an Australian summer. The two girls have just started their first year at school. Emma is not quite five years old. Hannelore is a few months older, the child of a German academic who is employed by the local university. Emma's parents are both professional people. The girls are bright, alert and winning. Both have entered school knowing a lot about literacy even though neither can yet read and write. We selected them for inclusion in our study because it appeared, on the basis of interviews with them during the first week of the school term, that they were likely to learn to read and write quickly. We made video recordings of them at work during writing sessions at regular intervals over the full school year.

In the first set of recorded writing sessions, we asked Rhonda to give individual assistance to each of our six selected children in turn, but since the recording was done in the classroom under conditions which were as close to normal as possible, Rhonda also talked to other children who asked for her assistance during these sessions. Later, as the children became more proficient writers, Rhonda told us that they no longer wanted or needed her close attention, so we arranged for our selected children to sit together at the same table during the sessions we recorded so that we could capture how they interacted not only with Rhonda but also with each other.

Our predictions about Emma and Hannelore proved accurate. By year's end both girls were reading and writing. In the interviews at the beginning of the year they had been unable to read a copy of *The Three Bears* that we offered them, and when we asked them to write they produced only a list of a few words. Observations of them in school verified that they were indeed not readers or writers although they knew a great deal about books and print. By the end of the year they were able to read *The Three Bears* for us without difficulty and wrote a short, meaningful and coherent text without prompting or assistance. In this chapter we discuss their participation in the individual writing sessions in the first weeks of school, giving readers a sense of what the children knew and could do when they started school and what the teacher needed to do in order to get the children involved in learning to be writers.

At the Beginning

In the first three months of the school year Rhonda's intentions in her literacy lessons were global. Her primary objective was to provide opportunities for the children to learn how to participate in writing as an activity. She wanted them to learn the process of 'writing a story'. Producing conventionally correct texts was not of central importance. Being able to participate, no matter how limited the participation, would permit them to elaborate and refine their understandings of what it means to be a writer. If they were unable to participate, no learning could take place.

Beginning in the second week of school we recorded Rhonda working with each of the children we had selected for observation as they tried to produce a simple written text. At this stage the children knew very little about how to write a 'story', so it is not surprising that their conversations with Rhonda about their writing often ran into difficulty. These video recordings are valuable as a record of what the children knew and could do at the beginning of the school year. And because the sessions include frequent communication breakdowns we can see more clearly what the children still needed to know to be able to participate fully in conversations about writing, and what the teacher had to do to compensate for their initial lack of competence.

Learning to Talk about Literacy

Episode 3.1 was recorded at the beginning of the third week. Emma has already participated in six 'blackboard story' sessions. Rhonda has introduced a number of words to the class and they are on display in the Sentence Maker at the front of the room. She has also tried to make the children familiar with the other words on display in the room. Before the start of the episode Emma has, with Rhonda's help, decided on 'Stirling is having a birthday' as her 'story', but difficulties arise from the very beginning.

Episode 3.1

Rhonda: so what's the first word of your story?

Rhonda is looking intently at Emma's face but Emma looks down and does not respond.

Rhonda: what's the first word?

Emma makes eye contact, looks away and then re-establishes eye contact as she speaks.

Emma: Stirling

Rhonda: (nods) Stirling * so we have to write Stirling

Rhonda has continued to look directly into Emma's face. Emma looks away again.

Rhonda: so how would you **know** how to write Stirling?

Emma still avoids contact. Rhonda leans forward and lowers her head, seeking eye contact.

Rhonda: Emma

Emma still avoids eye contact.

Rhonda: how could you find the word Stirling?

Emma continues to look away across the classroom

Stirling stands up and walks towards Emma with his name card in his hand.

Rhonda: look out * I think Stirling's going to help us

Stirling places his name card on the desk in front of Emma who continues to look directly ahead.

Rhonda: look what Stirling's brought for you!

Emma looks down at the name card.

Emma: oh yeah

Rhonda: all right * can you write that?

Emma starts to copy 'Stirling' from the card.

StirlingEzHoTingEBDIrtt
doTHEEZ FiV.

Emma's completed text: 21st February

• Comprehension monitoring

Successful involvement in conversation requires the participants to monitor each other's behaviour and listen attentively to what is being said. When young children are involved, however, adults must assume most of the responsibility for detecting and dealing with comprehension difficulties, just as Rhonda does in the above episode. What happens in this exchange is typical of what happened in most of the early sessions. Rhonda watched the children's faces very closely as she spoke to them, often leaning forward and lowering her head to make sure that she could see their responses to what she said, and evaluate their level of understanding. If the child began to write, she would look at the page to see what was being written and then shift her gaze back to his or her face as soon as he or she had finished writing. The monitoring of response was close and constant.

Emma's behaviour in Episode 3.1 is not unusual. In everyday life children are not subtle. If they do not understand what an adult says to them their most usual response is to ignore the speaker. They look away and refuse to become involved. Emma behaves like this during this exchange with her teacher. She mostly avoids eye contact even when Rhonda lowers her head to make avoidance more difficult. She even persists in looking away when Rhonda speaks her name, something which would normally have a strong coercive force in the context of a classroom. This signals clearly that Emma does not understand what is expected of her. Even when the name card is placed directly in front of her she continues to avoid involvement. It is only when Rhonda explicitly directs her attention to the card ('Look what Stirling's brought for you!') that Emma looks at it and recognises what it is. Consequently their conversation about 'writing a story' is able to continue. Rhonda's persistent observation of and sensitive response to Emma in the episode is characteristic of both good communicators and effective teachers.

• Saying what is intended and understanding what is meant

Part of Emma's difficulty might be found in the differences in her experience of communication before and after entering school. Such discontinuities have the potential to create learning difficulties. Jenny Cook-Gumperz (1975) has observed that in the years before school the young child's interpretation of speech is *iconographic*. By this she means that

> the setting, shared history of the participants and presently occurring events for the participants are treated as a single communicative event in which verbal utterances and their prosodic features form a single unit for interpretation by the child. All parts of the message and context contribute *equally* to the possible interpretation. *All components are considered to contribute similarly to the understanding for both the child and his reciprocal partners.* (p.151 original emphasis)

At school, however, children have to recognise that some aspects of the communicative icon are foregrounded. What might be normally taken-for-granted or simply ignored is specifically marked and made part of the talk. For example, the type of speech event involved or the purposes of the talk might be explicitly stated so that what is being said can be properly interpreted.

In Episode 3.1 Emma identifies 'Stirling' as the first word in the story but seems not to know what to do next. The history of participation in writing activities which she shares with Rhonda is very limited. Her knowledge of the setting and the resources it offers for writing is also limited. The presently occurring events cannot be interpreted, then, in the light of experience or prior knowledge. Emma has only Rhonda's words to rely on, and those words often do not reveal in a simple and transparent way what Rhonda means.

Rhonda's reaction to Emma's lack of response is to try to make explicit the purpose of what is being done. Emma identifies 'Stirling' as the word to be written but makes no move to write it, so Rhonda says, 'in so many words', what the purpose of the activity is ('So we have to write Stirling'). By so doing she makes the immediate purpose of the activity a topic of the talk itself (i.e. the topic of the conversation explicitly becomes 'ways of writing Stirling'). This is a strategy she often used in the early part of the year while talking to the children about their writing, and it is fundamentally important. If the purpose of the activity is not clear there is little chance that participants will talk sensibly about what is going on, or that a successful outcome will be reached. But since Emma has had little experience of writing and knows almost nothing about how to attempt to write unknown words, making the purpose explicit, in this case, has no effect. Emma does not know how to attempt to write words which are not in her simple and limited written vocabulary so telling her that she has to write 'Stirling' does not help.

As we said above, in Episode 3.1 Emma has to rely on language as the primary source of meaning. This can create difficulties, not least because what is said is not always the same as what is meant. A question, for example, might not really be a question. The mother of a girl who is about to leave the house during heavy rain might say to her, 'Where's your raincoat?' and it would be a foolish child who treated that utterance as a question. She would understand that she was being told to get her raincoat and put it on. She would be able to interpret what had been said in the light of her understanding of the situation and her mother's customary ways of speaking in such situations. Her shared experience with her mother would play a crucial role in arriving at an appropriate interpretation of what her mother meant.

Context and Comprehension

Similarly, during Rhonda's conversations with the children about their writing, a question is not necessarily a question. In the above episode, when her explicit statement of the purpose of the activity draws no response, Rhonda asks two questions. First she asks, 'So how would you *know* how to *write* Stirling?' When that still fails to bring a response she follows up with, 'How could you *find the word* Stirling?'

It is not surprising that the first question brings no response. Superficially it seems to be a question about Emma's knowledge of writing. She might reasonably have answered, 'I don't know how to write.' But what Rhonda's question really means is that the written word 'Stirling' is available in the classroom, and that it could be found and copied. Every child has a name card and these cards have been referred to quite often in the early weeks. Rhonda is hoping that Emma will remember that these name cards exist and will see that they present a solution to the problem of 'how to write Stirling'. Emma does not make these connections.

Rhonda's second question ('How could you find the word Stirling?') is an attempt to make her meaning more explicit. When she says 'the word' Rhonda means 'the printed word. The question is saying, in effect, 'the printed word 'Stirling' is on display somewhere in our classroom. Find it'. Understanding this is no simple matter. Emma needs not just to be aware of the available resources for writing but must also know how to use them. She needs both to be aware of the name cards and to remember the occasions when they have been used in the construction of 'blackboard stories'. Emma fails to respond appropriately because she is not yet sufficiently familiar with either the situation (writing a story with her teacher's assistance) or with Rhonda's customary ways of speaking in such situations.

Constructing Context

In the last chapter we referred to Edwards' and Mercer's suggestion that it was the teacher's task to introduce children to the epistemological culture of the school '... by creating, through joint action and talk with the child, a contextual framework for educational activities'. The notion of 'context' as it is used by Edwards and Mercer, however, needs to be elaborated. Context, they say, is not something which is concrete for the observer but intersubjective for the participants (Edwards and Mercer, 1989, p.92). It is, therefore, an essentially mental phenomenon. Things 'out there', they say

> become contextual only when they are invoked – that is, referred to, assumed or implied in what is communicated. The very act of naming things, or of assuming shared understandings of them, makes their reality for communicators a social and conceptual one, rather than one of simple physical existence in the surrounding world. Context *is* the common knowledge of the speakers invoked by the discourse. (Edwards and Mercer, 1987, pp.160-161)

The physical circumstances surrounding any act of communication, they say, could support any number of descriptions and interpretations. But what matters is what the participants think has been said, what they think was meant and what they see as relevant. Even the surrounding discourse, they say, is only contextual to the extent that it is remembered or understood, whether accurately or not (p.66). The basic problem in Episode 3.1 is that, despite her best efforts, Rhonda fails to establish 'Stirling' as contextual. The clues offered by Rhonda, through her questions, fail to prompt Emma's memory of relevant experiences and information. Emma does not remember the name cards. Or, if she does remember them, she does not appear to see their relevance to the situation in which she finds herself.

The card is finally made contextual in the most direct way possible – by placing it on the desk directly in front of Emma and explicitly drawing her attention to it. It then becomes possible to establish mutual understanding and to achieve the intended outcome (writing 'Stirling' as the first word in the sentence). But not all of Emma's writing problems will be able to be solved in such a direct and concrete way. If Emma is to make progress as a writer she needs to be able to collaborate with Rhonda in the construction of intersubjective contexts based on shared memories and joint intentions. But both the understanding of intentions and the accumulation of shared memories takes time. In the following chapters we examine some of the ways this happened in Rhonda's classroom.

• Asking questions

The children would often avoid eye contact when they seemed not to understand but at other times they responded as Emma does in Episode 3.1. When she answers Rhonda's first question she doesn't just say 'Stirling'. She turns to Rhonda and makes eye contact as she says it. Even though no explicit question had been asked Rhonda recognises what Emma has done as a request for confirmation and she nods in response.

In any educational dialogue questions play an important part. While avoidance signals a complete lack of understanding, questions (even mute or implied ones) provide evidence of the child's involvement in the dialogue. Questions suggest that the child has entered a 'zone of proximal development', a point at which something might be achieved through dialogue which would not have been achieved independently. And if the children understand the purpose of the activity in which they are involved, and have at least a broad idea of how to achieve that purpose, their questions can indicate to the teacher precisely what they need to know. That makes the achievement of mutual understanding and the solution of problems much easier. Eventually, however, instead of just seeking confirmation, as Emma does in the episode above, children begin to ask for elaboration and specification of detail. They begin to engage more and more in the *negotiation* of meaning as their understanding of writing as an activity develops and the body of knowledge they share with their teacher grows. The frequency of questioning and the types of questions asked are an index of growth. They show to what extent the child is fully engaged in trying to arrive at mutual understandings with their adult partner.

Helping the Child to Learn

We agree with Barbara Rogoff (1990, pp.28-29) that '... the child and the social world are mutually involved to an extent that precludes them as independently definable'. And when we describe, separately, what either adult or child did in the sessions we recorded, we have tried, as she says she did, to ' ... define each person's actions with respect to the context provided by the other's actions, goals and circumstances'. Here we discuss what the teacher did to help the child, trying to make clear that:

a) the teacher's behaviour is always structured by, and responsive to what the child is doing

b) the context which is referred to as the basis for attributing meaning to utterances and actions is dynamic, flexible, and intersubjectively achieved – not something fixed and pre-determined

c) the teacher's purpose is to try to engage the child in goal directed joint thinking in the course of which she helps her to attend and think and remember so as to achieve mutually understood goals.

These general points inform the following account of what the teacher did to help the children to learn. At times we have to discuss teacher and child separately, but that should not be taken as an indication that the learning conversations discussed can be meaningfully separated into discussions of what the adult does, and what the child does, and what influence context exercises upon the talk and the learning that takes place. The conversations we discuss and analyse are unfolding events during which adult and child respond transactionally to each other and, in doing so, *create* the context which provides the interpretive framework which allows meanings to be negotiated and socially defined goals to be achieved. In Episode 3.1 we demonstrated that before such conversations can occur a body of shared knowledge needs to be established. In the next episode we look specifically at the types of things Rhonda did in the opening weeks of the school year to overcome the limitations of the children's experience and knowledge so that they could start participating in writing as an activity, and so begin to develop their competence as writers.

The first session involving Hannelore was recorded about two weeks after school commenced. In these individual writing sessions, Rhonda routinely asked all the children to 'write', but there was no expectation that they would actually be able to do so. Hannelore had shown no precocious writing ability. She had been doing much the same as the other children: drawing pictures, writing her name, copying classroom print and producing strings of letters. Rhonda does her best to maintain the conversation and to help the child to write her chosen 'story'. On this occasion she meets with more success than she did with Emma.

Episode 3.2

Rhonda has just sat next to Hannelore at her table. She makes eye contact and speaks.

Rhonda: what was it? I saw a mermaid?

Hannelore: in the water\

Rhonda: (nods as she speaks) in the water

Eye contact is maintained throughout this exchange.

Rhonda: well * what's the first word of your story?

She looks away briefly and then makes eye contact with Rhonda as she speaks.

Hannelore: I?

Rhonda: I * all right. (nods towards the page) I\

Hannelore writes 'I'.

Hannelore's 'Mermaid' text: 12th February

• Establishing a focus for discussion

Because one of the greatest problems in the early stages of learning to write is knowing what to write about, and how to frame what is to be written in appropriate language, Rhonda always made sure that the children had a 'story' ready to be written before the individual writing sessions began. Ten minutes before this episode was recorded Hannelore had framed such a 'story' with Rhonda's help. But it is only when Rhonda says, 'what was it? I saw a mermaid?' and Hannelore responds 'in the water' that the 'story' is established as the subject of the dialogue that follows. This is a prerequisite for understanding. It is only when both parties know unequivocally what the focus of attention is, that utterances within the context can be reliably interpreted and acted upon. Once the story is established as the joint focus of attention, meaningful discussion can take place about how to analyse and record it.

The pattern of discourse is common in classrooms. A teacher asks a question to establish a joint focus of attention (e.g. Can you see the flowers?) and then follows up with a directive or question about the object of attention (e.g. Bring me the yellow one). What is different in this case is that the focus of attention is not something concretely present but something recalled from memory; something which will need to be *retained* in memory throughout the entire session. A large part of Rhonda's effort during her dialogue with Hannelore in this session will have to be directed towards maintaining a joint focus of attention on this 'story'.

• Exposing the structure of the activity

The structure of the activity is marked clearly so that the children are fully conscious of the way it is broken into simpler sub-tasks to make it more manageable. For example, Rhonda often marks the transition points in the structure (as she does during 'blackboard story' sessions) with a boundary marker (e.g. all right) so that the children will be aware of when one sub-section of the activity has finished and the next started. In this sequence 'well' marks the boundary between stipulating what the 'story' is going to be, and identifying the first word that is to be written. Then, when Hannelore has done this, Rhonda marks the transition to writing the word by saying 'all right'. In effect she is saying, 'We've agreed on the word to be written. Now let's actually write it.' She uses these verbal boundary markers regularly (though not invariably) in her dialogue with the children during writing sessions. The deliberate highlighting of the sub-stages helps the children to be conscious of the structure of writing and therefore, ultimately, to be able to use it deliberately in writing their own stories.

• Making participation easier

The language and situation in this exchange between teacher and child are similar to the familiar routines of the 'blackboard story' sessions. When Rhonda asks, 'Well, what's the first word in your story?' this is almost identical to the way she phrases her questions during the 'blackboard story' sessions. Experience of group story construction and word search activities complements and facilitates the children's participation in individual exchanges with their teacher about their writing.

• Helping the children to show what they know

Although Hannelore correctly identifies the first word in her story she does not make an immediate attempt to write it. She needs Rhonda to prompt her with a nod at the page and a repetition of the word which is to be written. This is not exceptional. Young children frequently display what cognitive psychologists call a 'production deficiency'. The fact that she does not spontaneously demonstrate her competence does not mean that she is not competent. She just requires Rhonda's intervention before she displays her competence. Children like Hannelore and her classmates often need adults to help them to attend and remember in purposeful, goal-directed ways and this will continue to be true even as they become more proficient as writers.

• Acting as 'consciousness for two'

Jerome Bruner (1986) discusses the research he did with David Wood and Gail Ross which investigated ' ... what actually happens in a tutoring pair when one, in possession of knowledge, attempts to pass it on to another who does not possess it'. What they observed was that Dr Ross acted as 'consciousness for two', performing functions for the children which they could not perform for themselves, and helping them to do things that they would not have done spontaneously. Rhonda's behaviour in the following episode illustrates, in part at least, what it means to act as 'consciousness for two' during interactions with children. This is from the same session as Episode 3.1. Emma's 'story' is 'Stirling is having a birthday.' The next word to be written is 'having'. Rhonda engages in the phonemic segmentation of 'having'. She has identified the first sound as 'huh' and, after a prolonged exchange involving the use of an alphabet chart, Emma has recognised H as the appropriate letter and has written it on her page. As soon as the letter has been written Rhonda moves straight on.

Episode 3.3

Rhonda: having * huh * huh-**a**

Emma makes eye contact with Rhonda.

Emma: A

Rhonda nods.

Emma leans forward as if to write and then looks up at Rhonda again.

Emma: how do you do an A?

Rhonda: A

Rhonda looks across at the alphabet chart on the wall and then turns to make eye contact with Emma again.

Rhonda: Emma * on the end of Emma

Emma: oh

Emma writes 'a'.

Rhonda is doing most of the cognitive work in this situation because Emma has not yet developed a strategy for story writing. She is holding Emma's place in the 'story' for her, and keeping in mind the complete sentence so that the goal is not forgotten. And she is breaking the task into more manageable sub-tasks. She maintains a focus on the spoken message because Emma cannot do that for herself at this stage, and then proceeds to analyse it for her. She not only identifies the next word in the 'story' for Emma but also engages in phonemic segmentation of it.

When Emma produces the required letter name but discovers that she does not know how to write the letter, Rhonda behaves differently. She directs Emma's attention and cues her memory by saying ,'On the end of Emma.' Rhonda is building upon something she knows Emma knows; her own name. But the name is also physically there on her name card on the desk. This time Rhonda is not doing what Emma cannot do. She is helping her to do things within her competence that she would not do spontaneously.

One other thing is also worthy of comment. Although we focus mainly on the changes that occur from one writing lesson to the next, usually several weeks apart, each writing session is itself an unfolding event during which changes occur. In Episode 3.1 Emma had to be prompted to write 'Stirling'. But ten minutes later, when Rhonda offers the cue, 'Emma, on the end of Emma' the child writes 'a' spontaneously. It seems that she is a little more aware that the purpose of the sessions is not just to identify the words and letters but to write them. Where Rhonda had to act as 'conciousness for two' in the writing of the word 'Stirling', Emma has now taken control of that small part of the task. Emma is learning.

• Responding contingently

On the basis of a series of research studies started in the 1970s, David Wood (1975, 1976, 1980, 1988a, 1988b, 1989) concluded that effective teaching depends on contingent response to children. The general objective of such teaching is to sustain the children's involvement in the learning activity by offering just as much support as is needed to maintain effective engagement in the task. Wood has written that

> Contingent teaching ... involves pacing the amount of help children are given on the basis of their moment-to-moment understanding. If they do not understand an instruction given at one level, then more help is forthcoming. When they do understand, the teacher steps back and gives the child more room for initiative. In this way the child is never left alone when he is in difficulty nor is he 'held back' by teaching that is too directive and intrusive. (1988, p.81)

Wood says that in the 'real world' of the classroom contingent instruction is far more difficult, but because Rhonda spent so much time talking to children individually, even when the camera was not focused on her, contingent response was the norm. We see an example of this in the episode below.

Episode 3.4

In this sequence 'birthday' has been identified as the next word to be written. Rhonda has first tried a general prompt to write ('Come on, birthday'). Since that has failed she now tries something more specific.

Rhonda: where are we going to get birthday from? * now you want the word birthday * like where I wrote it on the board this morning

Emma looks towards the chalkboard and Rhonda follows her gaze.

Rhonda: birthday ** can you see it?

Emma continues to look at the chalkboard but looks blank.

Emma: no I can't see it very properly

Rhonda speaks to Charles.

Rhonda: could you go and get the word birthday for her? ** sit down Emma * he'll get it for you * it's hard for you to see that far isn't it?

Emma: yeah (nods)

Charles brings the card to Emma.

Rhonda: here's birthday.

Rhonda's first attempt to get Emma to write 'birthday' is a general verbal prompt. When this fails to draw a response she asks a question ('Where are we going to get 'birthday' from?') which offers more specific information. This is the type of question Rhonda asks during joint story constructions and word search activities. She would have hoped that Emma might understand it to mean that the required word was somewhere amongst the print in the classroom and that she should search for it. Rhonda is watching Emma closely so that when there is no response to this move she provides further help. She reminds Emma of a shared experience involving the writing of 'birthday'. This provokes a response. Emma looks towards the chalkboard but when Emma's responses tell Rhonda that she is still unable to follow her instructions she provides even more help by asking one of the other children to bring Emma the card with 'birthday' printed on it. All that remains is for Emma to copy it.

This is typical of the way Rhonda responded to the children. She exercised progressively more control over their learning when they seemed not to understand. On the other hand, when they were able to proceed independently she withdrew and passed control to them, as she does in the next episode. When Episode 3.5 was recorded Emma had been at school for twelve weeks. She is writing about her mum. So far she has written

ym mum is prettyshe is A doctr

Rhonda has made no attempt to correct 'my' or to point out that spaces should always be left between words. Emma is making good progress and these matters will be left until later in the year. At the beginning of the episode Emma is in the process of writing another sentence: 'She goes to work.' So far she has written 'she'. Rhonda identifies the next word for her.

Episode 3.5

Rhonda: she **goes** ** **guh**

Rhonda lowers her head trying to make eye contact.

Rhonda: guh

Emma looks at the alphabet chart on her desk.

Emma: guh for ** **girl**

Rhonda: that's right (nods)

Emma looks at the chart for three seconds.

Emma: G!

Emma writes 'g'. Rhonda speaks as Emma is finishes.

Rhonda: she * **goes**

Emma makes eye contact. Then she stands and looks towards the Sentence Maker at the front of the room. Rhonda follows her gaze.

Emma: oh yeah * I know the word go

She turns to Rhonda and re-establishes eye contact.

Emma: G-O

Rhonda: (nods) that's right

Emma's completed text

Emma writes 'o'. As she finishes Rhonda speaks again.

Rhonda: go-**ssss**

Emma writes 's'.

Rhonda is still doing much of the cognitive work for Emma. She helps her to keep her place in the text and segments the next word for her. But Emma looks at the alphabet chart without being prompted and provides her own cue when she is trying to establish which letter represents 'guh'. Rhonda makes no attempt to interfere. As long as Emma seems able to proceed purposefully, she makes no effort to intervene. She lets the child take over. Emma then remembers that she already knows the word 'go'. In fact, what she means is that she knows where to *find* the word, not that she can write it spontaneously. Rhonda watches while she finds the word in the Sentence Maker and then, when she is asked, confirms that Emma has got it right. Finally Rhonda identifies the next phoneme for Emma who promptly writes the appropriate letter.

Rhonda's contingency of response involves offering whatever help Emma needs on the basis of a moment by moment interpretation of her behaviour. She attends closely to everything that Emma says and does, and responds in terms of whether the child seems to understand what is expected of her but her interpretations of Emma's behaviour are not made exclusively on the basis of what she observes during this particular session. Rhonda is aware of the group experiences of the class. She is also aware specifically of what Emma knows, and what Emma might be expected to do, in what is now a familiar situation, after three months experience of schooling. This is no research laboratory. Contingency in communication is based on what the participants know about each other as well as what they know about communicating. It is an important factor in the success of the literacy instruction in Rhonda's classroom, and it makes it likely that even the briefest exchange with a child is likely to lead to the development or refinement of what that child knows or can do.

Communication and Learning

We have already agreed with Edwards and Mercer's statement that teachers have the responsibility for establishing, '... through joint action and talk with the child, a contextual framework for educational activities' (1987, p.161). We have shown in this chapter that establishing such a framework requires considerable effort on the teacher's part because it is often the case that children initially know so little about the things the teacher wants to talk about and so find it difficult to become involved in the conversational exchanges that are fundamental to learning. Communication under any circumstances can run into difficulties. It involves much more than the ability to produce grammatically well formed sentences. It is a two-way process. Communication can only be said to be taking place when something which is said, or done, brings a response (Gumperz, 1982). But in the episodes we have discussed so far the children sometimes failed to respond and made their non-involvement in the talk very clear by refusing to make eye contact and ignoring what was said to them. When this happened there seemed to be little prospect that the child would learn anything from the encounter. Rhonda Fisher, like many other excellent teachers, nevertheless persisted in trying to find areas of common knowledge upon which mutual understanding could be established. She knew intuitively that children who are not communicating are having difficulty in learning, and that such children need, above all, the assistance of adults who do all they can to maintain communication with them.

Some of the reasons for failures of communication in the classroom are easy to identify. For example, while adults are mostly free to choose whether or not they will take part in a particular conversation, after drawing inferences about what the interaction is about and what might be expected of them if they choose to participate (Gumperz, 1982, p.1), children in school are usually coerced into conversations about things the teacher thinks should be the subject of discussion. It should not surprise us, then, if they show few signs of involvement early in the year when their teacher attempts to draw them into conversation. We should not, however, conclude that what Rhonda was doing in the early sessions was futile. As we will see in the next episode, taken from the same session as Episode 3.2, recorded about two weeks into the school year, even at the earliest stages genuine negotiations of understanding between teacher and child can take place if the circumstances are right.

Episode 3.6

The last word in Hannelore's text is 'water' and she has decided that it finishes with the letter T. Rhonda has accepted this and helped her to find 'T', using the alphabet chart which is pasted inside her writing folder on the desk. Hannelore finishes copying the letter T from the alphabet chart.

Rhonda: and then is your story finished?

Hannelore: yes

Rhonda lowers her head and looks into Hannelore's face. Hannelore looks past Rhonda.

Rhonda: well what happens when the story's finished? ***

Hannelore makes eye contact.

Hannelore: I write a new one

Rhonda: yes yes well what **finishes** a story?

Hannelore breaks eye contact.

Hannelore: full stop

She starts to insert a full stop at the end of the first line. Rhonda is watching.

Rhonda: full stop * well **that's** not the end of your story.

Rhonda shakes her head.

Rhonda: where's the end?

Hannelore looks up at Rhonda. Rhonda looks up as well and makes eye contact. She nods at the text.

Rhonda: where's the end?

She nods in the direction of the text again. Hannelore looks down and away from the text. Rhonda maintains her focus on Hannelore's face and nods towards the text again.

Rhonda: after the last word * which one's the last word that you just wrote?

Hannelore continues to look down but she shifts her gaze to her text and puts the point of her pencil to the right of the last letter she wrote.

Rhonda: **that's** the end of your story (nods)

Hannelore inserts the full stop.

• Becoming involved

Earlier in the writing session from which this episode was taken, there were points in the conversation when Hannelore withdrew from involvement because she clearly did not know what was expected of her. In this episode, however, she continually signals her involvement by what she says and what she does. We can see in this the influence of Rhonda's efforts to prepare the children for conversations about their writing. It is mainly through involvement in the joint story constructions (during which Rhonda routinely asked questions like, 'Is our story finished?' and 'what do we do when we finish a story') that Hannelore has been introduced to the use of full stops. As the episode shows, she does not fully understand how they are used, but it requires only a little overlap in knowledge to permit Hannelore's initial involvement in this conversation with Rhonda. Once involvement has been achieved, a fine-tuning of Hannelore's understanding of the use of full stops becomes possible. Without involvement no further development is likely.

• Misunderstanding and not understanding

If learning is to take place, becoming involved in conversation is essential. And once involvement is achieved participants need to continue actively to signal their involvement. But involvement is not enough in itself. It is just a precursor to understanding. Once the conversation starts, the more knowledgeable participant, responding contingently, helps the less competent participants to understand what is being said. Communication difficulties will naturally occur, especially when the asymmetries in knowledge are marked, but if such difficulties are recognised they are usually dealt with promptly and the conversation moves towards mutual understanding.

In Episode 3.6 two types of difficulty with understanding occur: misunderstanding and not understanding (Bremer *et al.*, 1996, pp.37-41). The 'story' to be written was clearly stated at the beginning of the session as 'I saw a mermaid in the water.' At the beginning of the episode Hannelore has just finished writing 'water' (which she has spelled 'wrtot'). Rhonda's first question ('and then is your story finished?') means 'Have you written everything you said you wanted to write?' The next question ('well what happens when your story's finished?') means, 'Well, if you've written everything that you intended, how do you show that you've finished?'

But Hannelore has interpreted Rhonda's first question as meaning that her 'story' is complete in every detail. So it is not surprising that she does not understand Rhonda's question as it was intended to be understood: that is, as an indirect request to insert a full stop in her still-to-be-completed text. Instead she responds in a way which is consistent with her interpretation ('I write a new one'), and which exposes her misunderstanding. Rhonda responds by re-phrasing her question so that it is framed in much the same way as the questions she has asked during the 'blackboard story' sessions. This makes it possible for Hannelore to place the question in an appropriate interpretive framework and she replies, correctly, that a full stop is needed.

What she does next reveals not a misunderstanding but a lack of understanding. Hannelore moves immediately to insert a full stop in the text, but in doing so she shows that, while she might know what full stops look like, she does not yet understand how they are used. Rhonda recognises this problem instantly and begins a process of negotiation that ultimately leads to the full stop being inserted in the appropriate place in the text.

• Negotiating understanding

So Hannelore knows what a full stop looks like, and she knows that one has to be placed in her text somewhere. What has to be resolved is where to put it. When Hannelore starts to place the full stop at the end of the first line, Rhonda immediately recognises the nature of her difficulty and says, 'well that's not the end of your story'. This utterance is intended to do two things: to stop Hannelore from putting the full stop in the wrong position and to tell her indirectly where it should be placed. It succeeds in achieving the first outcome but not the second. Hannelore knows that she has got it wrong but does not understand that she is to put the full stop at 'the end of her story'. She does nothing. Rhonda responds by asking, 'Where's the end?' This is really a request for action, which means, 'Show me the end of your story.' Hannelore still fails to respond, possibly because of the elliptical form of the utterance. Had Rhonda been more explicit ('Where's the end of the story?') Hannelore might have understood what she was being asked to do. She turns and makes eye contact with Rhonda, perhaps seeking elaboration, but Rhonda only repeats her last question. This suggests that she thinks Hannelore had not heard the question clearly the first time. At this point Hannelore looks away, not only from Rhonda but from the text as well. She has withdrawn from involvement. This prompts Rhonda to increase the explicitness of her guidance. She says, 'After the last word.' Once again she is telling Hannelore where the full stop is to be placed, except that she is now more specific. The end of the story, she is telling Hannelore, is after the last word. Then, increasing the pressure for a response from the child, she asks, 'Which one's the last word that you just wrote?' This is even more explicit than identifying what is needed as the *last* word. What is required is the last word *written* in the text *which has just been completed.* The target item could hardly be more unambiguously identified. And once again the question is really a request for action ('Show me the last word that you just wrote'), something that Hannelore clearly recognises because she responds, not by saying anything but by pointing at the end of the last word in her text. She waits for Rhonda's confirmation of the adequacy of her response and then, without further prompting, she inserts the full stop at the appropriate point in her text.

Rhonda could have achieved the same outcome by simply pointing to the end of the sentence herself and saying, 'Put the full stop there'. But she did not, because she knew that to be successful at school children have to learn to focus on language as the chief source of meaning. Hannelore is learning not just the use of full stops but how to engage in such things as the establishment of joint attention and the negotiation of reference in the discussion of written language texts. It is not just writing that is the focus of learning, even in these early sessions, but the practice and refinement of the communication processes themselves. Hannelore shows that she is equal to the demands being made of her although she has experienced less than fifteen days of formal schooling. And this suggests that what Rhonda has been able to do is create circumstances in which Hannelore could employ and refine her pre-existing communicative competence in the pursuit of new goals.

But what is perhaps most important of all in this episode, is what Hannelore has learnt about learning. She might seem to have made little progress towards becoming an independent writer but she has gained valuable experience in learning collaboratively with her teacher. And it is growth in her capacity to learn to solve problems in co-operation with others which will be the critical factor in her growth both as a writer and as a learner generally.

• Communication and learning difficulties

In this episode (indeed, in most conversations) both the child's misunderstanding and her lack of understanding were detected and dealt with immediately. In many classrooms this does not happen. Lack of understanding often goes undetected. Misunderstanding is frequently not noticed. This means that the lack of understanding is not resolved and the misunderstanding is not cleared up, and the basis for further learning difficulties is consequently established. We believe that learning difficulties (including difficulties with reading and writing) are much more likely to result from such unrecognised and unresolved communication difficulties than from any deficiencies in children themselves. So when children display difficulties in understanding, the first thing that should be done is to ensure that teachers are being sufficiently responsive to the children's signals that they are puzzled or uncertain. This is the only way to prevent future confusion being built upon today's lack of understanding.

The one-teacher-to-many-children ratio in classrooms might seem to make the detection of problems in understanding difficult, but the episode above shows why this need not be so. Hannelore needed only a little knowledge to become involved in a discussion of full stops. That knowledge came from her participation in carefully planned whole class lessons. But once she became involved in conversation with Rhonda, what she said and did demonstrated her current level of competence and what she still needed to know. On this basis Rhonda was able to respond to the exact difficulty Hannelore was having. We can be sure that at the end of the episode Hannelore knew a little more about full stops than she did at the beginning. And the whole exchange lasted less than two minutes.

This is not to say that Hannelore needed no more help with full stops. In the next session we recorded some weeks later she was using full stops confidently and correctly but we do not know how this happened. Learning sometimes involves a moment of insight; a sudden leap forward. At other times it involves a slow accumulation of experience; a gradual fine-tuning of understanding during a series of exchanges with people who know more than we do about what is being learnt. But regardless of how learning happens, long individual tutorial sessions are usually not needed. In classrooms like Rhonda's, in which the communicative framework for understanding had been carefully established, short exchanges like the one in Episode 3.6 assume enormous importance because they provide children with chances to test the hypotheses they have developed in whole class lessons in the company of a supportive adult who responds briefly but precisely to their demonstrated needs. If opportunities exist for frequent brief exchanges of this type, it is far less likely that problems with understanding will be missed and that serious learning difficulties will subsequently develop.

Starting to Learn About Written Language

• From phonemic awareness to understanding

In the first session we recorded, Hannelore was sometimes able to segment her stories into words but she had great trouble segmenting individual words into sounds. She could not yet consciously attend to a word's separate phonemes (i.e. the units of sound in the word). She seemed to be deficient in phonemic awareness; that is, 'the ability to explicitly separate and manipulate the separate sounds in words' (Andrews, 1992). In the view of many psychologists and educators, this deficiency is likely to create difficulties for a beginning reader.

Sally Andrews, for example, says that children first have to recognise that spoken words can be broken into phonemes before they can make use of 'the alphabetic relationship between spoken and written words'. Children who are not 'phonemically aware', she says, are forced to recognise each word individually and this is an inefficient strategy which will ultimately cause them to fall behind on measures of reading comprehension when compared with children who are able to engage in the phonemic segmentation of spoken words at the beginning stages of literacy development.

But 'cracking the alphabetic code' is just the beginning. Andrews says that it is also possible for children to develop an overreliance on alphabetic relationships which will cause them to 'have difficulty in spelling irregular words.' In order to become efficient readers children need to move beyond the 'alphabetic stage' into an 'orthographic stage' of reading development when word recognition no longer depends on single letters but on 'larger units such as letter clusters and morphemes'. Reading development depends upon extensive experience with words and word families. Children, Andrews says,

> need to have developed 'rich' memory representations of words that integrate their visual and phonological characteristics and allow the child to quickly and efficiently distinguish between similar words. If children are to achieve this stage, they need to experience words in isolation as well as in context. If a word is guessed from context rather than explicitly decoded, the child does not pay attention to the aspects of the word that crucially distinguish it from other similar words. (Andrews, 1992, p.91)

Children need to practise individual word decoding ' ... in order to develop automatic associations between the visual pattern of a word and its sound and meaning'. Once word meanings can be accessed automatically, Andrews says

> children are free to devote their attention to the high level processes required for comprehension. Phonemic awareness and decoding skills therefore provide the basis for the development of an efficient database and data-retrieval system on which later training in the 'thinking' components of reading can operate. In this sense, these low-level skills are crucial to efficient reading comprehension. (Andrews, 1992, p.91)

According to this view of reading development, phonemic awareness is a prerequisite for the development of decoding skills. Familiarity with the visual as well as the phonological features of words provides automatic access to word meanings. Automatic access to word meanings then permits the child to work on understanding written language. It is through these links that Andrews explains the causal relationships between phonemic awareness and the development of efficient reading.

• From understanding to phonemic awareness

Not everyone is convinced by such arguments. As we pointed out in the last chapter, David Olson (1996) has claimed that writing is not the transcription of speech but provides instead a model for speech. From this perspective, phonological awareness is not seen to be a prerequisite for reading. Instead, learning to write using an alphabetic script involves learning the model of language implied by that script. That written language model then provides a way of thinking about language, both spoken and written.

Although Rhonda herself would not have spoken about what she was doing in these terms, we believe that Olson's comments provide a plausible explanation for what we observed happening in her classroom. The capacity to use phonemic segmentation as a strategy for writing words grew out of the children's participation in joint story constructions through which they developed a capacity to think about speech as something which could be analysed first into words and then into sounds.

• Learning to control mental processes

Through their involvement in the construction of 'blackboard stories' the children in Rhonda's class were taught to listen to speech as if it was made up of sounds. But other things also needed to be learnt. Hannelore could recognise and name most of the letters of the alphabet and could identify the first 'sound' in a number of simple words when she entered school, but in the following episode (recorded in the first two weeks) she seems unable to engage in any phonemic segmentation of the word to be written (water) and to be struggling even with the identification of letters. Yet, with Rhonda's assistance, she is eventually able to find the required letter and copy it into her text. By prompting her memory Rhonda is able to help Hannelore to use what she knows. Hannelore would appear to be in a zone of proximal development, but *what* is being developed?

Part of the answer to that question is that she is developing an awareness of the activity of her mind (Vygotsky, 1986). To understand what is happening in Episode 3.7 we have to recognise that the focus in the exchange is not on individual word decoding but on the development of Hannelore's control over her memory through dialogue.

Episode 3.7

This episode comes from the same session as Episode 3.2, recorded in the first two weeks of school. Rhonda is helping Hannelore to write 'water' by breaking the word into phonemes for her and then helping her to make grapho-phonemic matches.

Rhonda: wor- **tuh**

              wor- **tuh**

Hannelore looks up and makes eye contact with Rhonda as she speaks.

Hannelore: T

Rhonda nods three times.

Hannelore prepares to write, then hesitates and shifts her gaze to the alphabet chart in the folder which is open on the desk.

Hannelore: how do you write a T?

Rhonda looks at the chart.

Rhonda: like ** for train

Rhonda looks up at Hannelore's face. The child is still focused on the chart.

Hannelore: mmmm

Hannelore shifts her attention from the chart to her text. She points at where she has written 't' before. Then she writes 't'.

Rhonda is doing the phonemic segmentation for Hannelore. That is not surprising because it has been demonstrated that five-year-olds have great difficulty with such tasks. She also has to guide Hannelore in making the match between the phoneme and the corresponding letter of the alphabet. Rhonda has already helped her to find 'T' in the alphabet chart earlier in this session and Hannelore has copied the letter into her text. During the first search for the letter T, it was Rhonda who opened the alphabet chart and made it the focus of joint attention. She offered the same clue to its location that she offers in this episode ('like for train'), but on that occasion it was Charles who identified the letter, pointing to where it was displayed on the chart. Hannelore did not even have to recognise the letter. All she had to do was to copy it.

Hannelore is an intelligent and alert child so it might seem surprising that she appears to have no memory of how to write the letter after having found it in the alphabet chart and copied it into her text no more than ten minutes earlier. She asks here, exactly as she did a little earlier, 'How do you write a T?' But there is a difference.

On the second occasion Hannelore still does not recall the letter spontaneously, but she does respond more readily to the prompts she is given, and the exact nature of her act of remembering deserves close attention. When Hannelore names the letter she looks at the alphabet chart without needing to be prompted. She clearly remembers that this is *where* she found the letter T earlier. She remembers an incident she has personally experienced. That enables her to establish an appropriate focus of attention, something Rhonda had to do for her on the first occasion. Hannelore now has only to *recognise* the letter by distinguishing it from the others on display in the chart. She still cannot do this spontaneously but when she is given the picture clue this time she locates the letter rapidly. Recognition of the drawing of the train gives access to the required information. It is interesting that once she has identified the letter in the chart she then remembers where she wrote it previously. Seeing the letter triggers recall of where it is in the text. At each stage a further cue prompts more remembering.

It seems, therefore, that Hannelore solved her problem in Episode 3.7 by engaging in two acts of remembering. First, she remembered *where* to find the required information, an act of remembering apparently cued by saying the name of the letter. Next she found the letter in the chart, an act of recognition cued by Rhonda. That is, recall of a shared experience led to mediated recognition. The child's remembering is social in nature with Rhonda providing whatever support is needed, at each stage, to ensure that what is relevant to the solution of the problem is brought into focus in the child's consciousness. It also involves the use of joint knowledge of classroom-specific, shared experience. This is why it is so important that teachers engage the children in shared problem-solving. Remembering the shared experience permits the child to establish a focus of attention on information pertinent to solving the problem. At this stage in the year prompting the children's memory is a means to an end. It does not provide direct access to the needed information but rather a means by which the needed information can be found.

We have already pointed out that children of Hannelore's age do not necessarily use information or strategies they are known to possess unless they are prompted. Teachers have to persist for some time in reminding them of what they have experienced and what they have learned before they begin to use that knowledge spontaneously in response to problems they encounter. There are many examples of exchanges similar to this one in our data. It seems, then, that what Hannelore is learning in this episode is how to cue the recall of graphophonemic relationships for herself through the use of such concrete aids as alphabet charts. She is learning how to remember actively through the use of signs (i.e. the language cues and the alphabet chart illustrations), something Vygotsky (1978, p.51) has said is the very essence of human memory. At this stage Rhonda is generating the signs for Hannelore. Later she will do it for herself.

This is a process of learning which is very different to the one suggested by Andrews. This episode suggests that voluntary rather than automatic responses are being developed, and that remembering rather than encoding is the crucial aspect of the learning which is taking place. This learning is also fundamentally and essentially social in nature rather than isolated and individual; and it is arrived at through the negotiation of meaning, not through the decontextualised analysis of printed words.

• Fine-tuning existing knowledge

The next episode comes from the same writing session as Episode 3.1. Emma has nominated 'Stirling is having a birthday' as her story. Before the episode begins, Stirling has brought his name card to Emma's desk and she has copied the word 'Stirling' from it. Rhonda has then analysed the next two words into phonemic segments for Emma and helped her to find and copy a letter to represent each 'sound' in turn. At the beginning of the episode Emma has written 'Stirling es hav'. Rhonda identifies the next phoneme to be written as 'ing'. Charles is taking a great interest in what is going on.

Episode 3.8

Rhonda: we've got the 'vuh' * now we want the 'ing'

Emma does not respond. She looks blankly into the middle distance.

Rhonda: ing

She makes eye contact with Charles.

Rhonda: can you remember this morning in our story what said 'ing'?

Charles: ing.

He breaks eye contact.

Rhonda: ing * you remember

Rhonda notices Stirling's name card on the table.

Rhonda: oh ** Stirling!

She makes eye contact with Charles again.

Rhonda: like the 'ing' on the end of Stirling

Emma looks at what she has written.

Charles: ing * ing for England * yes

Rhonda: no * like an 'ing'

Emma points at where she has written Stirling. Because Rhonda has been trying to engage Charles in the conversation she does not notice.

Rhonda: ing

Emma: oh

Stirling's name card is partly hidden by papers and the folders on the desk. Rhonda picks it up and places it on the desk directly in front of Emma.

Rhonda: which bit would say 'ing'?

Emma: this bit.

Emma points at the beginning of the word.

Rhonda: no * that's the 'stirl'(She runs her finger under 'stirl') * ing * (she runs her finger under the 'ing' as both children look on)

Emma: oh yeah (she points at the end of the word with her pencil and runs it across the 'ing' and back again.) * those three letters

Rhonda:(Nods): those three letters * that's right

Bruner (1983) has said that 'fine-tuning' in spoken language acquisition is well illustrated in acts of reference. The mothers in Bruner's study first established joint attention on the object which was to be referred to and labelled. If necessary they restricted the degrees of freedom for the child so that joint attention could be established. The chief objective in the negotiation of reference, however, is to help the child to realise that a particular vocalisation 'stands for' the object of joint attention. Further, the mother tries to ensure that her infant recognises that there is a *standard* way of referring to whatever they are sharing visually.

The above episode involves the fine-tuning of Emma's understanding of the way grapho-phonemic correspondences can be represented in print, and what happens is very similar to the exchanges between Bruner's mothers and their infant children during the fine-tuning of their understanding of spoken language. When Emma seems unable to respond to Rhonda's early attempts to establish a joint focus of attention, Rhonda places Stirling's name card directly in front of the child. This establishes joint attention in an absolutely unambiguous way. There is no doubt what Rhonda's next question ('Which bit says 'ing'?') refers to.

The question also helps to make the act of reference easier to achieve. It takes the form 'Which one is the X?'. That is, when Rhonda asks which bit says 'ing', she is providing a category and asking Emma to indicate an instance, rather than showing her an instance and asking her to categorise it. Rhonda asks the child only to recognise, rather than name or define the target item.

When Emma still responds inappropriately Rhonda provides the label 'ing' while clearly indicating what she is referring to. She assumes that Emma understands what she means: that these letters 'stand for' the sound 'ing'. Emma's reply shows not only that Rhonda's assumption is justified but also in what respect Emma's understanding of grapho-phonemic relationships has been 'fine-tuned'.

Emma can recognise and name most of the letters of the alphabet already and she has shown in this writing session that she can sometimes match a phoneme to a corresponding letter. But what Emma has learnt in this exchange with her teacher is a new alphabetic principle: *one* sound can be represented by a *group* of letters. Her existing knowledge of the alphabet and of grapho-phonemic correspondences has been transformed by this new realisation. And she has learnt this through collaborative participation in an act of writing, rather than through the analysis of isolated words.

Conclusion

We have made it clear that we believe that learning is a social process and that it depends for its success on effective communication. Effective communication, in turn, depends upon a body of taken-for-granted knowledge and assumptions shared by those involved. Given that we were observing five year old children talking to their teacher about writing during the first month of the school year it is not surprising that some communication difficulties occurred which threatened to impede the children's learning. We saw what the teacher did to ease the children's introduction to learning to write, and how teacher and child worked together to solve the problems that occurred during the production of written language texts. What happened in this classroom resembles what Barbara Rogoff (1989) has called 'guided participation'. Guided participation, Rogoff says, has the following features:

• providing a bridge between familiar skills or information and those needed to solve a new problem

We noted that young children often display 'production deficiencies' and have shown how Rhonda helped the children to overcome these deficiencies by prompting them to draw upon relevant knowledge and skills which they possessed but did not use spontaneously. This is crucially important in promoting writing development in young children.

• arranging and structuring problem-solving

We also showed how Rhonda began to establish, from the first week of school, the structure of writing as an activity so that the children were clear about what they needed to do to be a writer in her classroom. This was achieved through their participation in the routine literacy activities of the classroom, especially the regular joint story constructions and word search activities. We also showed how she helped the children to deal with communication at school, involving as it did the foregrounding of language as the primary vehicle for meaning.

During the individual writing sessions Rhonda spent time with individual children, acting as 'consciousness for two', helping the children to attend, to plan and to remember until they were able to do these things for themselves. She helped individuals to solve writing problems by breaking the task of 'writing a story' into manageable sub-tasks and by helping them with aspects of the process (like the phonemic analysis of speech) which they could not manage for themselves at the beginning of the year.

• gradually transferring the responsibility for managing problem-solving to the child

We discussed some of the ways in which Rhonda responded contingently to the children, offering more help when they did not understand what was required of them, and withdrawing and passing control to them when they seemed willing and able to accept it. The basis of such contingency was close observation of the children so that responses might be made in terms of what the children were actually doing and the indications they gave of their understanding or their failure to understand. When the teacher detected signs of confusion she both simplified the situation for the child and provided as much support as was necessary to maintain the child's effective engagement in the task.

Communication and learning are inseparable. Failures to learn are more likely to result from the teacher's inability to maintain effective communication than from deficiencies in the children. If children fail to understand, it may well be that they are not sure what is being talked about or, worse still, that they believe that the talk is about something else. To make learning as easy as possible teachers should behave as Rhonda did, closely monitoring the children's understanding and responding to signs of confusion contingently until mutual understanding has been re-established. Children should be provided with whatever support they need to make their participation in the learning activities of the classroom possible, because participation is a prerequisite both for learning and for the development of voluntary control over mental processes like attention and memory. In the next chapter we look at the progress the children have made later in their first year at school and explain what made that progress possible.

Chapter 4

It is nearly seven months into the school year. Hannelore is writing about the Sports Carnival. She has just written that her team (Macquarie) won. Her actual text is 'MQOrie wun.' Emma, Claire and Damien, sitting at the same table as Hannelore, are also writing about the Sports Carnival. Damien looks at what Hannelore has written.

Episode 4.1

Damien: how did you spell 'won'?

Emma speaks to Hannelore.

Emma: no, not W * it's

Hannelore: not 'one' that's been like one person

(she holds up one finger)

MacQuarie won the game * something like that

Damien: (shakes his head) I know how to spell it * my mum told me
* it's the same as one two three four five

Hannelore: well I don't care

Hannelore is not pleased. She starts to write again.

Damien turns to Emma and makes eye contact.

Damien: it's true

Emma nods sympathetically.

Things have changed in Rhonda's classroom. For example, there is much more print. The pet show has been held recently and the children have painted pictures. Each one has a simple text attached, written by yesterday we had the Sports carnoM are Spoats carnovl we hadfun

I'm in TheBlue teeme it is cooled Meorie

and N I weVe are Blue teeShrt Meorie

we got the The moost poonts. My Meorie wyn.

Cheeringfor Mei muwn wos

Hannelore's 'Sports Carnival' text: 20th August

Rhonda: 'I'm Emma's dog' and 'This is David's cat' and so on. Every item on the Nature Table is labelled: 'Charles found this shell on the beach' and 'Claire brought this spider in for us to see'. There is a chart headed 'Rules We Must Know' and another which asks 'Do you know your colours?' On this chart the word 'red' is matched with a small red square; 'blue' is matched with a blue square; and so on. Yet another chart is headed 'Words We Know'. There are other charts with groups of frequently used words on them; for example, 'today', 'yesterday' and 'tomorrow'. The large Breakthrough to Literacy Sentence Maker is still on display at the front of the classroom and there is now a card for nearly every word printed on the folder. Some of the children's stories have been copied onto large sheets and attached to notice boards. Other 'stories' have been made into booklets for everyone to read. The shelves are filled with books and there are boxes of books on the floor. At the back of the classroom mothers coming in on a voluntary basis, read to the children individually and listen to them read. And all the other displays are still there: labels on doors and windows and desks; on the piano and the playhouse; the days of the week and the months of the year; an alphabet chart; numbers painted on the window; the children's name cards – and much more.

All the children are now attempting to write at least a simple sentence during the individual writing sessions. No-one is copying signs or producing random strings of letters any longer. Rhonda moves from table to table intervening when and where she thinks she is needed. Very few of the children now need or want her intensive support. There is talk but, as the above episode shows, the talk is often about what they are writing. Typically, the children sit back when they have finished a sentence and think about what to write next and perhaps look at and comment on what a nearby child is writing. They stop to listen to what Rhonda is saying to other children or what other children are saying to each other. Sometimes they call out the answer to a question Rhonda has asked a child elsewhere in the room, and they ask and answer each other's questions. But mostly the children are intent on writing, showing great concentration as they work.

Hannelore's complete text in this session was:

The Sports carnovl

yesterday we had are Sports carnovl we had fun.

I'm in the Blue teeme it is cooled MQOrie

and I were are Blue tee shrt MQOrie wun.

we got The moost poonts. my mum was

cheering for me.

This gives some indication of how far these children have come in less than seven months. Hannelore added 'ing' to 'cheering' when Rhonda made her conscious that she had omitted it, but the rest of the text was written without assistance. And as Episode 4.1 shows, the children are now discussing and even defending the decisions they make as they write. We now consider what has brought them so quickly to this level of competence.

Mastering the Activity Structure

The next episode was recorded at this time – seven months into the school year. Rhonda is sitting with a group of six children, including Emma, but she is not giving exclusive attention to any one of them. She is observing and responding. She asks questions about what each child is writing and answers the questions directed to her.

Rhonda is seated across the table from Emma. She has already asked some of the other children what they have chosen to write about. Emma does not wait to be asked.

Episode 4.2

Emma: I'm going to write about school.

Rhonda: about school? you're not going to write about going to David's?

Emma shakes her head and leans forward, ready to write.

- First she writes her heading 'School'. She says, 'ssss' and writes 's'. Then she remembers that 'school' is one of the words in the Sentence Maker at the front of the room, so she looks up and copies it.

Emma's 'School' text: 18th August

- Next she writes 'at', saying '**atuh**' as she writes 'a' and then '**atuh**' as she writes 't'.

- She then says 'at **school**' and looks at her heading. She writes 'school' without further reference to the word in her text, saying 'sss-kuh, school, school' as she writes it.

- She re-reads what she has written: 'At school. At school.' She pauses for three seconds and then says '**we**', writing the word as she says it.

- Then she says 'write' and looks up from her text before saying 'rr-ite.' As she says it she stands in her seat, leans over and looks at the front cover of her writing folder which has 'I Can Write Stories' printed on it. She stands and looks at this for fourteen seconds, speaking as she does so: 'Write ... rrr-ite ...W.' She then sits down and writes 'W' in her text.

- She copies the rest of the word letter by letter, saying the sounds or the letter names as she does so.

- She looks at what she has written and then reads it. 'At school we write...'. Then she refers to the folder again, saying '**stories**'.

- She copies 'stories', checking the word on the folder for each letter as she writes it. 'Ssss (writes 's') tuh (writes 't') sss-tuh(as she examines the word on the folder closely) stor (she writes 'o') stor (as she examines the word on the folder again) storrr (writes 'r') stor (as she refers to the word on the folder) storee (as she sits down and writes 'ie') storiesss (writes 's').'

- She sits back, looks at her text and re-reads it, tapping the words with her pencil as she reads them. 'At school we write stories.'

Emma now clearly understands and can reproduce the model of writing that Rhonda has offered them during blackboard story sessions. She analyses the spoken text word by word. She says the words as or before she writes them, finds and copies the words that are available in the classroom, engages in phoneme-grapheme matching and regularly repeats and re-reads what she is writing. She now knows what she has to do to be a writer in Rhonda's classroom.

Learning the activity structure of 'writing a story' is essential if the children are to learn to write but this is not enough in itself for the children to develop into fully competent writers. What is happening is not unlike what happens when some children are taught to play chess. First they have to learn the moves for each piece. Only then can they begin to participate. At first, however, many children play the game as if the objective is to take as many pieces as possible. Eventually, through repeated experiences of playing with a more knowledgeable partner, an understanding of the real purpose of the game is likely to develop. When that understanding is reached, and if the children continue to play, they might become part of the culture of chess, growing progressively more competent as they become aware of the way that other people, both now and in the past, have played and continue to play the game.

Like the novice chess player, Emma now knows enough to take part in the 'game' of 'writing a story'. To facilitate this Rhonda has provided something very much like the 'formats' which, as Bruner (1983) says, mothers provide for their infant children to make it easier for them to learn to speak. Like those formats, the 'blackboard story' allowed for the simplification and framing of input, and provided a basis for dialogue about an ongoing event, the construction of a written text. It was also scriptlike, being standardised in form and having slots for participation that the children were able to fill. In fact, it is language which constitutes and structures the 'blackboard story', mainly through the series of questions which Rhonda asks. And it is also language which directs the activity and which permits the outcome (the completed text) to be achieved. In the above episode Emma directs her own behaviour in a similar way, using much the same language that Rhonda regularly uses during joint constructions of stories on the chalkboard.

Emma has learnt enough about the structure and purpose of the activity, and about how to write the words she needs, to make it possible for her to participate in writing sessions in an acceptable way. And it is by continuing to participate in writing as an activity, in the company of other writers (Rhonda and the other children), that she will gradually refine her understanding of the purposes of writing and eventually become part of the broader culture of writing.

Writing the Words: Grapho-Phonemic Analysis

• Learning how to listen to speech

Emma and Hannelore both came to school knowing the names of most of the letters of the alphabet but showed little capacity to engage in the phonemic segmentation of words. At best they could identify the initial sounds of a few one syllable words. When they first attempted to write they needed Rhonda's assistance to make sound-letter matches and made frequent reference to an alphabet chart. In the first six months of school, however, through repeated participation in the literacy activities of the classroom, especially the joint construction of stories and the individual writing sessions, they developed the capacity '... to hear words as composed of the sounds represented by the letters of the alphabet' (Olson, 1996, p.86). The act of attempting to write texts with Rhonda's assistance focused their attention on what Olson has referred to as the 'segmental structure of language'. While they relied on Rhonda to segment the text for them at first, by the middle of the year they were often able to do this for themselves. They moved from knowing the names of the letters of the alphabet to understanding the model of language implied by that alphabet, just as Olson has suggested.

In the following episode, taken from a video recording made six months after the beginning of the school year, Hannelore is writing about a seal which she saw performing at the zoo. She has just written that the seal climbed up a ladder. She sits back in her seat. Rhonda glances down at her text.

Episode 4.3

Hannelore: and

Hannelore writes 'and' and then looks up. Rhonda also looks up to make eye contact.

Hannelore: jumped down off the top

Rhonda: he jumped down off the top did he?

Hannelore starts to write. Rhonda watches.

Hannelore: juh (she writes 'j')

Rhonda: jumped

Hannelore: uh (she writes 'u') mmm (she writes 'm') puh (she writes 'p') * jump

She looks up at Rhonda, who also looks up and makes eye contact.

Rhonda: jump**duh** * jumped (nods)

Hannelore: E-D

TArongu ZOO

we went to TAron gu zoo
he saw a Seal Show
nd Seal climd y up a lader
nto he jumped down and he Splash,
ve the wRater two more came ou
fed the Seals wyth figsh and we

Hannelore 10/7

went down and the Seal gave us a kiss
ind then we went to feel the baby
sharccks they were bumpy then we ha.
to go home,

Hannelore's 'Zoo' text: 10th July

Rhonda nods vigorously. Hannelore leans forward and writes the letters as she says them. Rhonda is focused on the text.

Hannelore: E * D *

She sits back and looks at what she has written.

Hannelore: jumped

Hannelore can now think about speech as being made up of sounds. She is able not only to segment the utterance into a series of words but also to analyse those words into constituent sounds and then match the sounds with letters. She did not arrive at this point by working through a set of phonemic awareness exercises or a highly structured phonics programme. Rhonda constantly involved the children in the phonemic analysis of words and phoneme-grapheme matching but did so in the context of group story constructions and individual writing sessions, not through the analysis of isolated words. She chose words for her 'blackboard stories' which gave her the opportunity to talk about particular features of words (for example, the difference between 'can' and 'cane'). And during Big Book sessions she drew attention to particular words because they illustrated some regularity (for example, words that rhyme) or because they were distinctive in some way (for example words with 'silent' letters). She would then refer back to these discussions and demonstrations when other stories were being written. 'Who can remember how we wrote 'having' in our blackboard story yesterday?' Or 'Who can remember seeing the word 'ghost'? What was special about it?' Rhonda was constantly aware of the things that the children needed to learn and the words they wanted to write, and she planned her blackboard story sessions and other literacy activities to provide opportunities to pay close attention to words and discuss their distinctive features. Learning about grapho-phonemic relationships in Rhonda's classroom was thus incidental but definitely not accidental.

We have seen that the various aspects of Rhonda's literacy programme were complementary. Each activity was part of a cohesive writing programme which was centrally concerned with developing each child's control over his or her own writing production system. Learning about the phonemic analysis of speech and sound-symbol relationships was therefore not an end in itself. The children were simultaneously involved in learning how such things fitted into the context of writing as an activity, and how the capacity to use grapho-phonemic knowledge was related to other aspects of the written language system.

Vygotsky's distinction between spontaneous concepts and scientific concepts helps to explain the nature of this learning. By spontaneous concepts Vygotsky (1987) meant those concepts which are acquired outside the context of explicit instruction. He also referred to these as 'everyday' concepts to signal that he did not mean that they had been spontaneously invented by the child. The children's awareness of print concepts and the letters of the alphabet at the point of entry to school were just such 'everyday concepts', developed incidentally through interaction with adults and perhaps through exposure to television programmes like *Sesame Street*.

By contrast, 'scientific concepts' are developed through instruction which reveals to the children the place of each concept in a system of interrelated concepts. In fact, it is only when concepts are understood as part of a system that they become subject to conscious control. If we apply this to a consideration of how children learn to write, it suggests that the children can only truly become writers when writing itself becomes the focus of attention and its systematic nature is understood. Knowing the names of the letters of the alphabet and even being able to attribute 'sounds' to those letters does not make a child a writer. Neither does an understanding of print concepts like 'letters', 'words' and left-to-right directionality. Before children become writers they have to understand how each of these things is related to the others in a system of written language production. But explicit instruction does not have to mean taking children through hierarchically organised sets of exercises. And it does not mean that children have to be 'taught' in order to learn. Effective instruction implies the involvement of children in purposeful, goal-directed, collaborative problem-solving in the course of which control is passed to the children as soon as they are able to accept it. The outcome of this type of instruction is a capacity to go beyond what is taught and to draw inferences and generate new understandings independently.

Vygotsky points out that scientific and spontaneous concepts do not exist in isolation from each other. Interaction between them is needed, he says, if 'true concepts' are to develop. The development of the 'true concept' demands not only the systematic framework arising from the learning of scientific concepts but also the 'growing down' of those concepts into relevant spontaneous concepts already in the child's possession. Learning the activity structure of writing as it was practised in Rhonda's classroom and, at the same time, developing a written language model which permitted children to understand speech differently, exemplifies what Vygotsky meant. The systematically organised written language model 'grows down' into children's pre-existing knowledge of spoken language, the alphabet and books, making them explicitly aware of what they previously knew only implicitly. This leads on to the development of conscious control which makes it possible for the children to analyse speech, to read analytically so that the internal details of words are noticed, and to produce written language messages independently.

• The role of memory in learning about grapho-phonemic relationships

Memory is always involved in learning, and a proper understanding of how these children became literate requires understanding the role of memory in their learning. According to Vygotsky (1978), when a person ties a knot in a handkerchief in order to remember something, this act transforms remembering into an external activity. The knot is a sign which the individual uses to control what is remembered. Remembering is no longer random but becomes deliberate. 'The very essence of human memory,' Vygotsky says, 'consists in the fact that human beings actively remember with the help of signs'.

The chief sign system used in this way is language and the greatest change in the child's capacity to use language to solve problems, Vygotsky tells us, occurs when socialised speech is turned inward. Instead of appealing to an adult, children appeal to themselves. We have already seen this process operating as Emma and Hannelore mastered both the activity structure of writing and an approach to writing words through phonemic analysis. We also see it happening in Episode 4.3.

In the last chapter we showed how Hannelore successfully identified the next phoneme in her 'story' as 'wuh' but then asked Rhonda, 'What's a wuh?' Being able to identify the sound did not mean that she could necessarily remember the corresponding letter. She depended on

Rhonda's help to make the match by reference to an alphabet chart. But when she spelled 'jump' by segmenting the word into phonemes and providing a letter for each sound, Hannelore was appropriating the role that Rhonda played in the early sessions. She no longer needed to appeal to Rhonda to name the sounds or to cue her memory of the matching letters or groups of letters. Naming the phonemes had become like tying a knot in a handkerchief. It externalised memory. The spoken phonemes acted as cues which prompted the recall of the matching letters or groups of letters. Once again it seems that the essential feature of Hannelore's learning, at this stage of her growth as a writer, is not the development of automatic responses but rather the development of control over the recall of information from memory through the voluntary and deliberate use of spoken cues.

• Learning to generalise about grapho-phonemic relationships

We have shown children learning to use phonemic analysis to write un-known words. This strategy is bound to lead to invented spellings. During the first months of the school year Rhonda rarely corrected an invented spelling of a particular word unless she knew that the child's attention had, at some time, been specifically directed towards the 'correct' way of spelling it or towards a generalisation which applied to it. If this was the case she would remind the child that the word had been discussed earlier. Reference would be made to a spelling 'rule' that had been demonstrated, or a new grapho-phonemic correspon-dence which had been dealt with, or a word group that had been dis-cussed, and a correction would be made. Here are some examples of how this happened.

Episode 4.4

Hannelore wants to write 'back' but has written 'bake'. Rhonda looks at her page and draws her attention to the written word.

Rhonda: why did you put E on 'back'?

Hannelore looks at the word and then up at Rhonda.

Rhonda: listen buh-a-cuh * if you put an E there what does it make the A say?

Hannelore: buh-ake

Rhonda nods as she speaks.

Rhonda: buh-ake * You don't want it to say 'bake' do you? You only want it to say 'back'.

Hannelore shakes her head and crosses out the 'e' leaving the word as 'bak'.

Rhonda is not concerned in this episode with teaching the conventional spelling of the word but with reminding Hannelore of a spelling generalisation that had been demonstrated a number of times on the chalkboard. Two things happen in this exchange. First, Rhonda reminds Hannelore of something she knows but has not applied to her writing of this word: that the 'silent e' on the end of the word indicates that it should be read as a long vowel rather than a short one. This is yet another illustration of a 'production deficiency'. Given the right support children show themselves able to do things which, at first, seemed beyond their understanding and competence.

Second, Rhonda draws Hannelore's attention to the impact of the way the word is spelled upon the *meaning* of what has been written. Hannelore is learning that the meaning of the word, and the context in which it is used, determine which written form is appropriate. Spelling is, then, not just a blind application of phonemic analysis. The spelling is determined by the meanings being expressed. It is clear, too, that the nature of the talk between Rhonda and the children is changing as they share more experience and knowledge. The teacher-child dialogue has become much more sophisticated, reflecting the development of the children's understanding of literacy, the growth of shared knowledge and changes in the teacher's expectations of what they might be able to understand and do.

In the next episode Rhonda focuses attention on something she chose to ignore in the previous one: the use of 'ck' in words like 'back', 'duck' and 'sick'. Emma has written that the fish in her story is 'sik'. Rhonda draws her attention to the word but Emma obviously does not know what she is expected to do and does not respond. The word 'duck' has been drawn to the children's attention in a Big Book session so Rhonda asks all the children, 'Who's seen 'duck' **written**?' There is no response.

Episode 4.5

Rhonda:	you didn't tell me * who's ever seen 'duck'?
	Damien have you ever seen 'duck'?
Charles:	I've seen 'duck'
Rhonda:	duck ** something about the 'c'
Charles:	yes
Rhonda:	*sometimes*
Charles:	*C-K*
Rhonda:	yes

Emma makes eye contact with Rhonda.

Emma:	C-K?
Rhonda:	yes

Emma adds 'k' to her word.

Another child says 'C-A.'

Rhonda:	No. Sometimes some words that have a cuh in them have C-K because that's a cuh too

Rhonda refers the children to a word that they have seen *written*. This is once again an appeal to the children's memory of events they have personally experienced and shared with her. Significantly, this reference is to the appearance of the word rather than the way it sounds. Only Charles can remember the word, and when Rhonda gives an indication of what she is after he immediately shows that he is capable of not only recalling the word but analysing it as well. Charles was not cleverer than the other children. Different children remember different things and Charles knows how to answer this question. In this instance his knowledge is what is needed. At other times other children remembered what Charles could not. Rhonda encourages the children to pool their knowledge and to assist each other. The good sense of this practice is evident in this episode. Remembering in this classroom is often jointly achieved and, consequently, what is available to the children is a collective rather than an individual memory of items and events. Joint thinking and collective remembering are amongst the most notable characteristics of this classroom.

In the next episode we see again that frequent drills and extensive worksheet practices are not an essential part of learning to use spelling generalisations. Rhonda is working with Charles, Amy and four other children at the same table. In her recent blackboard story sessions she has deliberately introduced words which provided the opportunity to talk about adding 'ing' to the ends of words. She notices that Charles has written 'haveing'.

Episode 4.6

Rhonda: what do you do in 'having' when you add 'ing'?'

Amy: you leave off the 'e'

Rhonda speaks to all the children at the table.

Rhonda: yes remember ** if you have 'e' on the word and you add 'ing' you drop the 'e'

Charles crosses out the 'e' in 'haveing'.

A little more than a minute later Amy leans across to attract Rhonda's attention.

Amy: I'm going to write coming and leave off the 'e'

Rhonda: good

Rhonda reminds the children about a particular demonstration she has recently given on the chalkboard. This time Charles does not remember but Amy does. Rhonda makes sure that all the children at the table are aware of the change Charles has made to the word, and again states clearly the principle behind the change. A little later Amy shows that she truly understands the 'rule' by applying it to a different word. Her ability to state the rule suggests that she has probably brought it under voluntary cognitive control.

In this episode Rhonda once again helped the children to remember past experiences relevant to a problem which needed to be solved. Their growth as writers will be measured in terms of how independent they become in such matters as remembering grapho-phonemic generalisations. Increasing competence will be reflected in the development of voluntary recall through the use of self-generated cues. In this episode Amy can use the principle when she is reminded of it. The ultimate test of her learning will be whether she will be able to prompt her own memory of the rule when next she needs to use it.

• The development of self-regulation in the use of grapho-phonemic knowledge

We have claimed that learning is an essentially social process. The social nature of learning in this classroom is evident in the next episode, which is taken from the writing session during which the target group was writing about the Sports Carnival. These children are clearly not isolated learners. Offering and seeking advice are obviously natural parts of their problem-solving behaviour. At the beginning of the episode Hannelore leans across the table and offers Emma advice about how to write 'carnival'.

Episode 4.7

Hannelore: just write 'car' and then 'N'.

Emma promptly follows this advice. Hannelore has already written 'carn' herself. She now turns to Claire who has finished writing 'carnival'.

Hannelore: how did you say you spell carnival?

Claire:　　　　C-A-R-N-O-F-L

Hannelore looks down at Claire's text and then writes 'ofl' as she says the names of the letters.

Hannelore: O-F-L

She sits back and looks towards the front of the room.

Hannelore: Carn-i-vuh ** vuh

She changes the 'f' to a 'v' in her text. She sits back again.

Hannelore: V *** carna

She looks over Claire's shoulder at her story and points to 'carnofl'.

Hannelore: Look 'vuh' not 'fuh'

Hannelore has become very confident about her ability to analyse words into sounds. She offers advice to both Emma and Claire about how to spell 'carnival'. What is most interesting, however, is the way she checks what Claire has told her against her own analysis of the spoken word, and then corrects it according to that analysis. This is one further indication of the confidence with which Hannelore is now using phonemic segmentation and phoneme-grapheme matching as a strategy for writing. But it also shows that she is now capable of self-regulation, at least in this aspect of her writing. She is reflecting upon the process of writing itself.

Conclusion

David Wood (1980, 1988b) has referred to a phenomenon which he calls 'the recognition-production gap'; the fact that children can recognise satisfactory outcomes before they 'assemble the means for achieving them'. He goes on to say that the recognition-production gap provides opportunities for intervention in the learning process. The effective teacher, he says, provides understandable demonstrations of outcomes in order to draw the children into the pursuit of the goals the teacher has set. One of the features of Rhonda's 'blackboard stories' was that the children soon became aware of what the outcome of 'writing a story' was meant to be. After a very short time at school they could recognise a 'story' when they saw one. On the other hand it took some months before they developed a clear plan of operation for writing a story themselves.

After seven months at school both Emma and Hannelore were closely reproducing the model of writing that Rhonda had offered them in the 'blackboard story' sessions. They were familiar with the steps involved in producing a written language text: framing a 'story' in written language form; identifying each word in turn and writing it; and regularly re-reading the developing text. They now had a plan of operation for 'writing a story'. But as well as learning the broad activity structure of story writing which made participation in the activity possible, they also gradually learnt strategies for writing words. For example, by the middle of the year the children had become proficient in the phonemic segmentation of words and no longer had trouble in making sound-letter matches.

This development was not a consequence of intensive instruction in phonics or involvement in a phonemic awareness programme. In fact it might be that, as David Olson (1996) has suggested, ' ... writing is not the transcription of speech but rather provides a conceptual model for that speech'. During 'blackboard story' sessions Rhonda involved the children not only in segmenting the 'story' into words but also in analysing some words into their component sounds. By so doing she was providing a conceptual model of writing that showed the children how the alphabet could be used to provide analytical categories which could be applied to speech. It seems to us that this understanding of the written language model came first and that the ability to use phonemic segmentation as a strategy for writing words came afterwards. After six months of school Hannelore could invent spellings for any word she needed – as her story on the sports carnival shows. Emma was equally proficient in this respect. In one session she exclaimed, 'I can write stop' and then wrote 'sdop'. Like Hannelore she had mastered the alphabetic principle.

At the same time Rhonda was making the children aware of spelling rules and new grapho-phonemic correspondences. She was making them conscious of the fact that there are standard ways of producing written language texts and conventional ways of spelling words. In order to understand fully how the move towards conventional forms in writing developed in this classroom, however, we need to look beyond phonemic segmentation and consider how the children's knowledge of their print environment influenced the growth of control over written language. It is to this matter that we turn in the next chapter.

Chapter 5

We were in Rhonda's classroom for three years. In the first year one of the children was an engaging five-year-old called Ruth Biddle. During the year Ruth developed a problem with her eyes and it became likely that she would need to go to hospital for treatment. This concern began to appear in her writing at school. In one writing session, for example, she wrote the following story:

> If I dont wer My glussss in school I will
> haf to go to HossBiddle

In time she did go to hospital. When she returned to school she wrote

> I went to Hospidol it was fun mum came
> to I culerdin Miss Fishers stensls

Not long after this Ruth was writing yet another story about this traumatic but exciting experience. We noticed that this time she had spelled 'hospital' conventionally. We asked how she knew how to spell the word. 'I saw it in a book,' she said.

Ruth's first hospital story

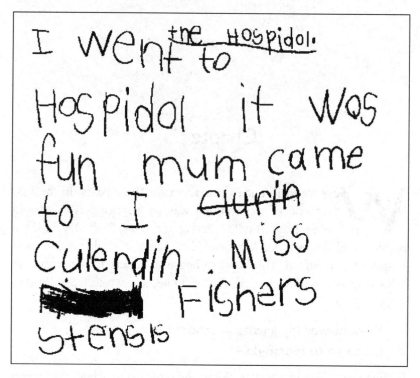

Ruth's second hospital story

In the two years of observations that followed, many of the children said things like, 'We wrote it once' or 'I always see it in books' when they were asked where they had unexpectedly picked up conventional spellings of words. It seems that producing a number of invented spellings of a specific word makes children more likely to attend closely to that word when they see it in books or on a wallchart in the classroom and, consequently, to notice its distinguishing features. Having mastered the alphabetic principle, the children begin to attend spontaneously to the details of how words are written and so develop more conventional ways of writing.

It has been claimed that explicit decontextualised decoding of words is necessary if children are to be able to distinguish between similar words and develop 'automatic associations between the visual pattern of a word and its sound and meaning' (Andrews, 1992, p.91). Our data, however, suggests that it is not decontextualised word analyses that lead the children towards recognising and using conventional forms of written language. In Rhonda's classroom it was a mixture of incidental instruction, engagement in the production of invented spellings and joint remembering which helped the children to develop control over conventional ways of writing words. In this chapter we look closely at the ways in which this happened.

Using the print environment of the classroom

In the last chapter we discussed what Rhonda did to develop the children's competence in the use of grapho-phonemic relationships. We have suggested that they first learnt the written language model primarily through their participation in 'blackboard stories'. This permitted them to 'hear' spoken language as being composed of 'sounds'. Once they began to hear speech as being made up of sounds which could be represented by letters of the alphabet, their pre-existing knowledge of the alphabet could be used within the systematic framework of written language practices. This led to competence in the analysis of speech and its representation in terms of grapho-phonemic relationships, but not to competence in the conventional representation of written words. The children frequently used invented spellings.

In moving the children towards conventional spelling, Rhonda's behaviour was much the same as when she was trying to develop their control over the use of grapho-phonemic relationships in writing. As she shared Big Books with the children, or constructed stories with them on the chalkboard, she drew attention to certain words and phrases, perhaps because they were commonly used or because they were distinctive in some way. For example, in one Big Book session she drew attention to the fact that stories often began with 'once upon a time'. In another she drew attention to the spelling of 'ghost'. She also made sure that the children were aware of the new displays of print around the classroom. She would, for example, ask them to read from the 'published' stories displayed on the notice boards and conduct searches for words on newly displayed charts. Later, when particular words were needed as the children wrote their own stories, she would refer back to the occasions when they had been discussed in class. In other words Rhonda was once again using memories of group experiences to help the children write the words they needed, rather than simply telling them what to do. When a child encountered a problem in writing a word Rhonda's underlying, unarticulated question was, 'What do we already know that will help us to write that word?' Her effort was directed at teaching strategies for remembering, rather than trying to develop 'enriched' mental representations through the analysis of words in isolation and by building word groups. She asked, 'Where can we find that word?' or 'Where have we seen that word?' or 'Who do we know who can spell that word?' or 'Who can remember when we wrote that word?' She constantly appealed to the memory of not just the individual but the group. Joint remembering and collective reconstruction were the experiences that provided the basis for individual development.

i) Assisted remembering

From the beginning of the year Rhonda tried to make the children aware of the print displayed in the classroom so that it would be potentially available to them when they needed to know how to write the words in their stories. But as we saw in the previous chapters, five year old children are limited in their capacity to attend and remember systematically (Flavell, Miller and Miller, 1993; Wood, 1988a). In the first weeks of school, both Emma and Hannelore failed to remember letters and words written only a little earlier in the writing session. In the episode below (recorded five months into the school year) Emma's capacity to recall information is still obviously limited. She cannot remember where she has seen 'because' despite the fact that she has already found and copied the word less than fifteen minutes earlier. But that does not mean that she has made no progress.

Episode 5.1

Rhonda: we've written 'because' once before

Emma immediately refers to her text, reading through it and pointing at each word in turn. She puts her finger on 'because'.

Emma: there's because

She starts to copy 'because' from the text. Suddenly, she looks up and points at the chalkboard.

Emma: oh yeah * it's on the board

And it is, in Rhonda's 'blackboard story'.

This episode differs from the one recorded at the beginning of the year. On this occasion, when Emma is reminded that she has written the required word only a short time before, she immediately fixes her attention on her text. She knows much more about writing and words and can now attend to the indicated source of information when given no more than an indirect verbal cue. Then, having attended to her text, she reads through what she has written, pointing to the words as she says them until she locates the one she needs. The words on the page are signs which externalise memory. They cause her to remember what has been written. She also controls her attention by pointing at the words as she reads them. Taken together, the written words and the act of pointing help her to control her mental processes so that she can find the word she wants to write. So although she is not yet independent as a writer, Emma is much better able than before to exercise voluntary control over her mental processes. In particular she is developing control over her memory and attention. At this stage, however, she still needs adult assistance to set in motion the processes by means of which she overcomes her difficulties.

It is interesting that, as she begins to copy 'because', she remembers that it is also written on the chalkboard. This further demonstrates the adventitious nature of remembering for Emma. Her remembering is governed by whatever enters her field of consciousness. Before she can be fully independent of adult assistance she needs to be able to control her own remembering; to generate for herself the memory cues which will bring to mind the information she needs to solve the problems which confront her.

ii) Incidental remembering

The next episode is similar in many respects to the last one. Hannelore has been at school for nearly seven months and she is now very aware of the words which are available in the classroom.

Episode 5.2

Hannelore has decided that 'Yesterday we had a sports carnival' is to be the first sentence in her 'story'. She leans forward and prepares to write.

Hannelore: yuh

> She seems as if she is about to engage in a phonemic segmentation of 'yesterday'. Then she swings around in her chair and refers to a chart on the wall. She reads from the chart.
>
> **Hannelore:** Today. Tonight. Tomorrow. Yes
>
> She turns back to her page and starts to write 'yesterday' referring frequently to the chart and saying the letters as she writes them.

'Yesterday' was a word commonly featured in the children's stories and this chart was often used to check how it was spelled. Hannelore had used it before. And yet it was only when she started to write the letter Y that she remembered where the word 'yesterday' could be found in the room. It seems, perhaps, that little has changed from earlier in the year, but that is not so. Although remembering that 'yesterday' could be found on a chart in the room was not a voluntary act of thought, it did not require an adult to prompt the child's memory. Hannelore initiated the thought processes that produced the cue that caused her to remember where to find the word. After this, what was involved was an act of recognition very much like the one Emma engaged in to find 'because'. Hannelore read down the list, saying each word distinctly, until she located the one she wanted. Then she copied it into her text.

The fact that Hannelore managed this for herself is almost certainly a consequence of Rhonda's frequent reference to, and use of, the words on this chart during literacy sessions. What Hannelore remembered was the personal experience of using this specific chart with 'yesterday' printed on it: an episodic memory. It seems probable that Hannelore often used her memories of participating in regularly occurring events like 'blackboard stories' and 'word searches' to help her to remember the general locations of the words she needed, so that all that was then required was an act of recognition. Once the right chart had been found, all that was needed was to decide which word among those on display was the one she needed. Such a strategy, derived from social interaction and based in personal experience, seems to be the means by which she overcame the limitations of recall typically found in young children. It is a strategy that permits children to behave as if they can recall the words independently until they actually can.

iii) Independent remembering

The next episode was also recorded seven months into the school year. Emma wants to know how to spell 'come'.

Episode 5.3

> Emma looks towards the Sentence Maker at the front of the room where 'come' is displayed. She cannot find it. She turns to Charles.
>
> **Emma:**   How do you spell 'come', Charles?
>
> Charles doesn't respond but Damien does.
>
> **Damien:**   C-O-M-E
>
> Emma writes 'come', saying the names of the letters as she writes them.
>
> **Damien:**   I don't even have to look to spell 'come'.

Two things are notable in this episode. First, Emma asks for help. She doesn't know how to spell the word she needs, so she turns to someone who does. She knows that the sources of information in the classroom include other children, and she initiates action to solve her own problem. She is no longer waiting for her teacher to prompt and guide her.

Second, we witness the outcome of repeated use of the words on display in the classroom. Damien previously needed to check in the Sentence Maker to see how to spell 'come' but now no longer needs to do so. This is consistent with the patterns of remembering which we referred to in the last section. The children first seem to remember the general location of the target word. This act of remembering is often connected with memories of incidents involving its use. Then, when the general location has been found, all that remains is that the word has to be recognised. This means that it has to be distinguished from other words in the same display. Finally, when it has been recognised, it is copied. At first these processes need to be set in motion by prompts from the teacher. Eventually the children can clearly be seen prompting themselves. Finally, after an unspecifiable and no doubt variable number of occasions of finding and using the word, the children can spell the word 'without even looking' just as Damien does.

The World of Books

At the same time that they were learning about writing the children were simultaneously being given reading experiences. Every joint story construction and Big Book session included individual and group reading, and during the individual writing sessions the children read and re-read what they were writing. Rhonda also 'published' some of the children's 'stories'. She printed them clearly in conventional spelling and made them into booklets or displayed them on notice boards in the classroom. Rhonda ran periodic sessions in which the children would be called upon to read their own and other children's stories.

Rhonda also regularly introduced new books by reading them to the class and talking about them. Although she chose books which she thought would appeal to the children and which they might be able to read for themselves, she made no effort to assess the readability of the texts or present them in a graded order. After they had been read to the class, the books were made available and the children made their own choices about what to read. These books came from the school library and other sources within the school. They included books from reading schemes but most were non-reading scheme story books and factual texts. Small copies of the Big Books were also available. The mothers who came into the classroom not only read these books to individual children but also listened to them reading from the same texts.

i) Finding words in books

The growth in the children's knowledge of books and their awareness of what books contained was another aspect of the growth of a body of common knowledge and shared experience in the classroom. By the second half of the year Rhonda frequently used this shared knowledge as another source of information about how to write words. In the next episode we see one way in which this often happened. Hannelore has written that the seal at the zoo 'splashed down into' and now has to complete her sentence by writing 'the water'.

Episode 5.4

Hannelore: the (she writes 'the')* wuh (she writes 'w')*

She hesitates and then turns to make eye contact with Rhonda.

Rhonda: water * wuh (nods)

Hannelore looks down at her page.

Hannelore: orrr *

She writes 'e', hesitates and then makes eye contact with Rhonda again.

Rhonda: wuh-orter water

Hannelore breaks eye contact.

Rhonda: wuh-orter

Hannelore writes 'e'. Rhonda looks around the classroom.

Rhonda: ummm/ * water ** ummm *** where can we see water? (she looks around the classroom again) *** let me think * what books have we got 'water' in? * water * (she turns to Hannelore) do you remember reading any books about water?

Hannelore suggests *Billy Balloon*, one of the Big Books that has been read frequently. When they look at it together, however, they discover that what Hannelore remembered was not the word 'water' (which is not in the book at all) but an illustration of a puddle. Rhonda then goes across to the book shelves and returns with *The Carrot Book* which she puts on the desk between them as she sits down. Hannelore opens the book and starts to turn the pages saying, 'Water. Water. Water.' She stops and looks at a page. Hannelore lifts the page so that Rhonda can see more easily and points to the print as she reads.

Hannelore: water the seeds

She turns to Rhonda. Rhonda responds and eye contact is made.

Rhonda: (nods) every

Hannelore's finger is still on the page. She looks down and reads on.

Hannelore: wuh * every day

Rhonda moves the book so that Hannelore can see it easily while she is copying from it. Hannelore looks closely at what she has written.

Hannelore: I'll cross that out (she points to where she has written 'we' instead of 'wa')

She doesn't look up but Rhonda still nods.

Rhonda: all right

Hannelore copies the word.

This time, when the efforts at phonemic analysis break down, Rhonda decides to use the books in the classroom as a source of information. Hannelore first recalls an item which is semantically consistent with the word she wants but in a different modality (visual art rather than writing). Rhonda, behaving contingently, intervenes by establishing a concrete focus of attention. She places *The Carrot Book* on the desk in front of the child. The illustrations in the book help Hannelore to find a page which has the word 'water' in the text. She reads the relevant phrase and points to the words as she reads them. Both the written language context and the illustrations play a role in what is predominantly an act of recognition. It is also interesting that Hannelore turns very readily to Rhonda with non-verbal requests both for assistance and for confirmation that she has found the right word. The whole episode is much more interactive than the ones in Chapter Three because Hannelore now shares with Rhonda not only a much greater knowledge of the print environment but also of the purposes of the activity and the processes involved in negotiating meanings. She is able to suggest a possible source of information. She holds the page up so that Rhonda can focus more easily on it, thus actively contributing to the maintenance of joint attention. And she comments on what she is doing (changing the 'e' to an 'a'), showing that she is aware of the purpose of the activity and that the processes involved are under her conscious control.

This episode shows how books added greatly to the stock of words potentially available in the classroom. But their efficient use depended upon two things. First, Rhonda's knowledge of the children: she had to know not only which words the whole class might be expected to have seen but also the words particular children might have read or written that were not known to the class at large. She had this knowledge because she was constantly involved in talking to individual children about their reading and writing. The teacher's expanding knowledge of the children (that is, the world of experience she shares with them) is as important to efficient communication and learning as is the child's expanded awareness of the print environment. Second, Rhonda is still responding contingently to the children, providing assistance when it is needed and withdrawing when the children are able to proceed independently.

ii) Remembering words in books

Of course the children eventually became independent of Rhonda and controlled their own acts of remembering. But being able to remember spontaneously has a history, as the next episode suggests. Charles is writing a story which begins 'once upon a time'. He has started to write when Rhonda sees that he has not written 'once' correctly.

Episode 5.5

Rhonda: well once upon a time * how do you spell once?

Charles makes eye contact with Rhonda.

Emma: O-N-C-E * O-N-C-E

Charles: O

He starts to write.

Emma: N-C-E

Charles finishes writing the word.

Rhonda: (to Emma) how did you know how to spell 'once upon a time'?

Eye contact is made.

Emma: because I ** I always ** I always look in books.

She points towards the books as she speaks.

Rhonda: so now you just know (Emma nods) how to write it all by yourself.

When we looked through Emma's writing folders we found that she had written several stories beginning with 'once upon an time'. In the early ones her spelling was unconventional, but once she had established how the phrase was spelled it remained consistently correct. Emma's behaviour again follows the familiar pattern. First came the attempts at phonemic analysis as a strategy for writing the phrase. Then she remembered (or was prompted to remember) the fact that the phrase she needed could be found in familiar story books. Next she started to use books to guide her in spelling 'once upon a time'. When this was done often enough Emma was simply able to recall how to write the phrase. Sometimes she said the phrase aloud in what looked like a self-generated memory cue. Usually she said each letter as she wrote it. Once again this looks like a strategy for keeping the word and its component letters in mind as they are written. Eventually she could write 'once upon a time', 'without looking' *or* speaking.

It appears that these acts of learning do not involve the development of automaticity of response. Instead, the children seem to be developing an increasingly sophisticated control over attention and memory. Such control grows out of social exchanges in which an adult first does the attending and remembering for the children. Over a period of time, however, the adult passes control to the children as they seem able to cope with the problem-solving demands of the situation.

Of course, not all words were learnt in this way. Some were learnt very early in the year using Breakthrough to Literacy materials, or were brought from home. These words were consistently spelled conventionally. Others seemed just to be picked up. When asked how they had learnt to spell a particular word some children told us 'I saw it once' or something similar. This did seem to be the case. The spelling of a word was sometimes remembered after only one exposure to it.

Nevertheless, the process outlined above was a common one, and the teaching strategies Rhonda used, which led to the development of the children's use of books as a source of information about words, were efficient and effective. These practices seem to have helped the children to become self-scheduling learners who, when they wanted to know how to spell a word, often remembered where they had seen it, checked its spelling and copied it. Copying and checking is a process teachers often encourage as a way of learning to spell in older children. Rhonda taught these children to use the strategy from the very beginning of formal literacy development, using books (and classroom charts) as the source of information against which the words were checked.

Gaining Control Over Topic Choice

i) Writing in the safety zone

Because of the decontextualised nature of written language, its uses and purposes are not immediately apparent to children. They have to learn what to write about and what written language can be used for.

To help her children with these problems Rhonda talked about interesting, shared experiences which provided topics for writing, and during the 'blackboard story' sessions she demonstrated ways of writing about them. For example, she wrote blackboard stories about current events at school: the pet show, the sports carnival, school excursions and so on. It is no accident, therefore, that these topics occur so frequently in the children's writing. Nor were the stories the children wrote unconnected with other classroom experiences. One of the Big Books read with the children was *The Magic Fish* and many children subsequently wrote stories about magic fish and magic butterflies and so on. Rhonda also wrote letters and jokes during joint story constructions and some of the children followed her lead. She encouraged the most advanced to re-tell, in written form, stories like *Jack and the Bean Stalk* and *The Three Bears* which had been read to them at school as well as at home and which could be found in the class library. Close to Christmas most children wrote letters to Santa Claus inspired by Rhonda's example during a 'blackboard story' session. By choosing such topics the children were able to write within safe boundaries. They could choose to write sentences similar to the ones already written by other children or by Rhonda and many of the words they needed for such texts were available in the classroom.

ii) Writing about things that matter

Rhonda provided ideas for writing but she did not impose topics. This is important because discovering which topics are worth writing about is an essential part of what is learnt. The sudden blossoming of truly personal writing in the children we observed was always a pleasure to witness, and what they wrote about was often a surprise. One of the children who was not chosen for special attention provides a striking example of what we mean. Bronwyn had been at school for just over three months. On the 5th May she wrote

> **I like to watch television at home and at school my mum and dad like to watch television. I can jump.**

This is a particularly turgid example of 'safe' writing. Every word is spelled correctly because each is on display in the classroom and has been carefully copied. This is writing intended simply to meet the perceived demands of the classroom. On the 9th May she wrote

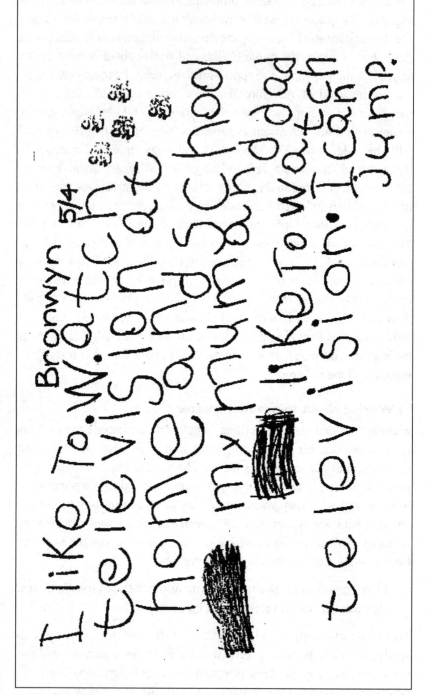

Bronwyn: Text One

> my mum is going to a Fenrel
> Blacs dad did I'm sad andef
> my mum is nt going Shesgo ing
> to looc rftur Blac.

Such occasions marked the emergence in the children of a sense of what writing is really for, and an insistence on writing about the significant events in their lives. Safe topics and safe spelling have been abandoned, giving way to the need to write about something which matters. This is a dramatic example, but these breakthroughs occurred in every child's development as they discovered the power of written language as a means of expression and a way of thinking. And it only occurred because they were genuinely given the freedom to choose what they wrote about.

iii) Writing and Reflecting

The next episode is less dramatic but it does demonstrate how emphatically the children learnt that they genuinely had control over what they chose to write, even when Rhonda was less than enthusiastic about their choice of topic. It is taken from a session six months after school began. The writing session has just started. Rhonda no longer needs to help the children to frame a 'story' but her 'blackboard story' for the day was about the Pet Show and she anticipates that many of the children will write about that. She sits down at the desk next to Hannelore and looks at her.

Episode 5.6

Rhonda: what are you going to write about Hannelore?

Hannelore looks up at Rhonda and makes eye contact.

Hannelore: about the zoo

Rhonda: about the zoo

Rhonda looks down and writes.

Hannelore: again * Taronga Zoo

She focuses on Rhonda's face and then down at what Rhonda is writing.

Rhonda: again * you're not going to write the pet show? ******

Hannelore looks up at Rhonda.

Hannelore: we went to the zoo and we saw a seal show

Rhonda looks up and leans forward as Hannelore speaks and makes eye contact.

Rhonda: well all right (nods)

She looks down again and recommences writing. Hannelore looks down at what Rhonda is doing.

Hannelore: and you could see this part of it

Rhonda: all right\ what are you going to call it?

Hannelore: I was going to *

Hannelore looks up at Rhonda.

Hannelore: no-one's allowed in except the people who work
                there * you give the seal a fish

Rhonda: do you?

Rhonda makes eye contact and then looks down again.

Hannelore: and you bend down it gives you a kiss

Hannelore stays focused on Rhonda. Rhonda looks up and makes brief eye contact as she speaks.

Rhonda: oh * so you're going to write about that?

Hannelore: yeah

Hannelore looks away and reaches for a pencil and prepares to write.

In this episode Hannelore, like Bronwyn, chooses a topic based on her life outside school. She has already written about her trip to the zoo on two previous occasions and Rhonda makes it clear that she would prefer her to write about the pet show but Hannelore persists. Her excitement about the experience is clear. She needs to write about it, not for anyone else, but because of its insistent presence in her memory. She resists Rhonda's pressure to write about the pet show, and even when Rhonda asks her what she is going to call her story she is not deflected. She persists in completing what she feels driven to say. This is no routine story. Since she must write, this is what she has to write about. She is writing to externalise what is occupying her mind.

And she is doing more than that. She is making her experience in the world the object of thought, and in writing about something which is outside the boundaries of safe topics, familiar sentence structures and easily located words, she is forced to focus on the act of writing in a new way. How can this exciting event be written about? Precisely what is to be said? And how are the new words to be written? The development of competence accelerates at times like this when the children, driven by the imperative of the things they must say, find new ways of using what they already know about writing.

Jerome Bruner (1986, p.127) has said that '...much of the process of education consists in being able to distance oneself in some way from what one knows by being able to reflect on one's own knowledge'. Intellectual growth, he says, is achieved by '...this process of objectifying in language or image what one has thought and then turning around and reconsidering it'. Hannelore's zoo story is an example of what he means. She is not just objectifying the event in writing. In texts like this we see the beginnings of reflection upon experience and the first step towards the development of a new form of consciousness. The child's focus is now moving from the mastery of the written forms to the use of written language as a tool of thought.

Writing About Fear

Here is another of Hannelore's stories. This time the experience which forms the topic of her text is frightening rather than exciting. She wrote it over a period of two days although it is by no means her longest text. It was finding what to say, the act of selecting and giving form to the experience, that took the time.

> once I had are nightmerre. I dydnt like
> it. it was so bad. I was crying in my
> dryem it was uBerwt fish in are pool. I fel
> into the pool. There were sharcs in the
> pooL. my friend Damian help me out.

This text is very different from the last. This is not a factual recount of experience in the world of parents and seals and trips to the zoo. This is about mental states: fear and panic and distress. Hannelore is not just writing a factual account of what happened in her nightmare – she is

once,I had are nightmerre. I dydnt like
it. it was so bad.I was crying in my
dryem it was yberut fish in are pool. I fel
into the pool. There were sharcs in the
pool. my friend Damian help me aut.

24/7 25/7

hannelore.

Hannelore's 'nightmare' text: 24th and 25th July

writing about how she felt. She is writing about the unconscious operation of her mind.

Almost all acts of writing involve remembering, selection and shaping. This is certainly true in this case. The chaotic experience of her nightmare is made concrete, given shape and form. Remembering it is one thing; writing about it is another. Writing this text was not just a re-construction of experience but a construction of meaning. Hannelore has constructed something she can control instead of it controlling her. In doing so, she has learnt still more about the relationships between writing and thought, and literacy and the emotions. Insisting that meaning can only be dealt with after the lower level grapho-phonemic 'skills' reach automaticity reflects a grossly inadequate conception of all the things that happen simultaneously as children learn to read and write. We are not just insisting on the primacy of meaning. Neither are we proposing a 'top down' rather than a 'bottom up' model of reading. We are asserting the essentially social, cultural and humane nature of literacy. And we are insisting that room should be left for the development of literacy in these senses from the earliest stages of formal schooling.

Gaining control over topic choice is obviously important in a number of ways. First, it can allow the children to regulate and control their own progress. Choosing familiar topics within their current competence allows them to gain confidence and consolidate what they know. Second, it provides the basis for using written language as a way of thinking; of objectifying experience and giving it specific forms. Finally, freedom to choose what you write about allows for the emergence of reflection upon personal experience, of not just reporting what has happened but making sense of it and thus gaining control over it – and that provides the means by which particular important forms of cognitive growth can occur.

Chapter 6

Referential communication research (Robinson, Goelman and Olson, 1983; Robinson and Robinson, 1985; Robinson and Whittaker, 1987a , 1987b) suggests that young children are not very proficient as speakers or listeners. They tend to interpret what is said to them in terms of what they think the speaker's intention is, rather than listening carefully to what is actually said. And when communication fails, the young child is likely to blame the listener rather than what was said, even if the message was obviously vague or ambiguous. It seems that children under six frequently fail to recognise that spoken utterances (both their own and other people's) might be ambiguous, and fail to recognise that what is said does not always reflect, in a simple and transparent way, what is meant.

David Olson has observed, however, that although the problem of sorting out the relationship between what is said, the intentions of the speaker in producing the message, and the interpretations that a listener can assign to it, is implicit in all language, it becomes central in dealing with written texts (Olson, 1986, p.155). This does not mean that pre-literate children are necessarily incapable of making these distinctions. Robinson and Robinson (cited in Robinson and Whittaker, 1987), for example, found that preschool children whose mothers sometimes gave them explicit feedback on the comprehensibility of what they said (e.g. 'I don't know what you're on about') were, at six, more advanced in their understanding of ambiguity than children whose mothers had not responded to their children in this way. But for most children, according to Olson, it is writing which '...brings into awareness the latent ambiguity of language' because it preserves language as an object which can be examined and analysed. When children begin to use written language they cannot avoid thinking about the need to be explicit in what they write.

In Episode 6.1, for example (recorded eleven weeks after school began), Rhonda focuses attention on the need to take account of how potential readers might interpret what is being written. Hannelore is writing about the cross country races which are to be held in the school grounds that afternoon. So far she has written

> we are Having The cross
> country today I amin Makqure (I am in Macquarie).

Episode 6.1

Rhonda reads the last sentence aloud, and then makes eye contact with Hannelore and asks her what else she might write.

Rhonda: and what else could you tell me? * what colour do they wear?

Hannelore looks directly ahead. Rhonda leans forward and lowers her head, trying to establish eye contact.

Rhonda: what colour t-shirt do you have to wear?

Hannelore makes eye contact.

Hannelore: blue

Rhonda: (nods) blue * well you could tell me we have to wear a blue t-shirt

Hannelore writes 'B'.

Rhonda: well not just blue * does that make sense?

Rhonda leans forward and points to the text as she reads it.

Rhonda: I am in Macquarie blue t-shirt

They make eye contact.

Rhonda: would that make sense?

Hannelore shakes her head.

Rhonda: no * so what do you think you could put?

Hannelore speaks hesitantly.

Hannelore's 'Cross Country' text: 17th April

Hannelore: the children in Macquarie wear a blue t-shirt

Rhonda nods encouragement as Hannelore talks.

Rhonda: good girl

In this episode Hannelore behaves like the children in the referential communication studies who seemed to be unaware that spoken utterances might be ambiguous. She seems to be unaware that her written message ('blue') might not be sufficiently explicit to convey her intended meaning unambigiously to potential readers. More detail is needed.

To focus her attention on the nature of the difficulty, Rhonda re-reads what has been written, adds what Hannelore is proposing to write and asks, 'Does that make sense?' She is not asking whether Hannelore knows what she means to say. She is asking whether Hannelore thinks that the word 'blue' alone would make sense to a reader. Nearly three months into the school year, Rhonda has begun regularly to ask such questions. She asks children to re-read what they have written and, if meanings are not clear, she asks them, as she asked Hannelore, 'Does that make sense?' This is a question that children have to learn to ask themselves. They have to learn to take into consideration whether others will understand the texts they are writing as they intended they should. This requires something new in cognitive terms. The children are being asked to think about other people's minds; about the ways in which they might interpret what is said or written. It is in such ways that becoming literate might be associated with the mastery of referential communication and the growth of communicative competence.

In the next episode, recorded six months into the school year, the topic for discussion is something different. The issue this time is not whether a reader would be able to interpret the text adequately but whether Hannelore has written exactly what she said she intended to write. This episode is taken from the session in which Hannelore was writing about her trip to the zoo. In her original account of what she intended to write she had said, ' You give the seal a fish and you bend down and it gives you a kiss'. What she has written up to this point in the writing session, however, is as follows:

Tarongu ZOO

I went to tArongu zoo
We Saw a Seal show
the Seal climd up a lader
and he jumped down and he splashd into the water two
more came out

Rhonda, as is her usual practice, asks Hannelore what else she might want write.

Episode 6.2

Rhonda: two more came out\ ** and then what happened?

Rhonda looks up at Hannelore's face but Hannelore just looks straight ahead.

***

Rhonda: Did you tell me you fed them?

Hannelore responds to Rhonda's question and makes eye contact. This is maintained for three seconds without either of them speaking.

Hannelore looks away. Rhonda leans forward and lowers her head in an attempt to make eye contact. As she speaks Hannelore looks up and re-establishes eye contact.

Rhonda: you didn't even feed them with a fish? or something happened *about them*

Hannelore: *we fed* * we fed them in a part that no-one's allowed to go in

Rhonda: oh

Rhonda nods towards the page and then looks up at Hannelore again. Hannelore is looking at her text. She moves her pencil back to the beginning of her story.

Hannelore: I think I've got it in here.

Rhonda: Oh well you read it through and see what you've got

Hannelore: we saw a seal show (she points as she reads) *** the seal ***

Rhonda: climbed/

Hannelore is still focused on the text.

Hannelore: climbed *** no we haven't got that

Rhonda: mmm? I can't hear you

Hannelore turns to look at Rhonda.

Hannelore: we haven't got that part

Rhonda: no we haven't

Hannelore looks down and prepares to write.

Rhonda: we've just heard about how he climbed up the ladder and jumped into the water

In Episode 6.1 Hannelore was asked to think about how others might interpret her text. In doing this she was taking early tentative steps towards the understanding that when producing written language, the text

> ... is separated from its own writer and open to an infinite range of readers and interpretations. In writing the author loses control over interpretation (cited in Olson, 1986, p.155).

No matter how carefully the text is worded, readers might still interpret it in ways never envisaged by the writer.

In this episode, however, the question is not 'Does it make sense?' It is: 'Have you left something out that you wanted to write?' What is at issue this time is intention rather than interpretation. Rhonda urges Hannelore to write about feeding the seal but the child hesitates. 'I think I've got it in here,' she says. Had she been discussing something that had been said rather than written, the whole situation would have been different. The spoken word is ephemeral. If no record is made of it, disagreements about what was said cannot be reliably checked, whereas writing makes language visible and permanent. Rhonda urges her to '... read it through and see what you've got.' Hannelore re-reads her text and then turns to Rhonda and says, 'We haven't got that part'.

Hannelore is learning that when questions are asked about a written text, the text itself can be used as a source of information. What is in the text provides evidence of what was said or, in this case, of what was not said. The text has an authority of its own. In such ways Rhonda was cultivating a new, literate way of thinking. Answers to questions of meaning can be found not just by reference to the world but by reference to text. The significance of this as an outcome of learning to be literate cannot be overstated. And the development of such habits of thought depends upon the way children are permitted to learn. Because Rhonda constantly urged her pupils to refer to and re-read their texts and check them for meaning and communicative adequacy, the children were learning not just to write but also about language, about ways of thinking about other people's minds and perhaps even about new ways of constructing knowledge (Olson and Torrance, 1987, pp. 165-167).

The next episode is also taken from the session in which Hannelore wrote about her trip to the zoo. She is trying to write the word 'were', which is on display in the large teacher's Sentence Maker at the front of the classroom. The Sentence Maker has two large cardboard leaves into which word cards have been slotted as the words were introduced to the class. It is these two leaves which are referred to as 'charts' in the exchange that follows.

Episode 6.3

Rhonda:　were

Hannelore: wuh (she writes 'w')

Rhonda:　were: (as Hannelore is writing the letter) it's like

Rhonda looks up. Hannelore responds and eye contact is made.

Rhonda:　um were

Rhonda turns around and looks towards the front of the room. Hannelore looks straight ahead.

Rhonda:　anyway it's up there * were

Rhonda turns to look at Hannelore and then back at the chart at the front of the room again.

Rhonda:　can you see the second chart?

Hannelore now turns to look at the chart. Both Hannelore and Rhonda are now focused on the chart.

Rhonda: am is are was **** were

Rhonda turns to look at Hannelore who has leant forward and is attending closely to the chart.

Rhonda: up the top

Rhonda turns to look at the chart again.

Hannelore: which one?

Rhonda: can you see it? look up the top

Hannelore: the second chart?

They are both focused on the chart. Rhonda points.

Rhonda: the second chart and look up along the top row * am is are **** was ** and then

Rhonda turns back to look at Hannelore, who is still fixed on the chart.

Hannelore: were * W-E-R-E

Hannelore points at the chart and turns to make eye contact.

Rhonda nods. Hannelore prepares to write. Rhonda looks down to watch what is being written.

Hannelore: E-R-E (she writes the letters as she says them)

She reads what she has written.

they were

When Rhonda initiates the search for 'were', she just looks in the direction of the appropriate chart. Hannelore does not follow her gaze, so Rhonda provides a verbal clue to the word's location ('anyway it's up there'). This is vague and ambiguous. There are many displays of words in the broad direction indicated by Rhonda. It is not clear which one is being indicated. Hannelore still does not respond.

Rhonda then turns towards the Sentence Maker and adds a more explicit clue ('can you see the second chart?'). This time Hannelore responds by looking towards the front of the room. Rhonda obviously assumes that joint attention has been established on the second chart because she reads the words across the top row to help Hannelore to locate the needed word. But although Hannelore is looking in the right direction she still fails to respond. Rhonda offers another clue, telling her to look at the top of the chart.

But Hannelore still does not know which chart she is supposed to be looking at. She asks, 'Which one?', meaning 'Which chart?' Rhonda, however, believes that joint attention has already been successfully established. She thinks that Hannelore is asking which *word* on the second chart is 'were', so she repeats her instruction to look along the top row.

At this point Hannelore realises that Rhonda has not understood her, so she asks specifically whether it is the second chart that is supposed to be the focus of attention. Rhonda, in turn, realises that Hannelore had either not heard, or not understood, her earlier reference to the second chart. She confirms that she is talking about the second chart and joint attention is, at last, achieved. Rhonda tells Hannelore again to look along the top row and reads the words again. Now that they are both looking at the same chart, Hannelore quickly locates 'were' and finishes writing it in her 'story'.

The conversations we recorded in Rhonda's classroom in the first two months of school were very one-sided. Because the children knew so little about writing, Rhonda dominated the interactions that took place as they tried to write their texts. The conversation in episode 6.3, however, is genuinely reciprocal. There has been significant growth in Hannelore's communicative competence. She is acting appropriately as both speaker and listener. As a listener she realises that she does not have enough information. As a speaker she realises that Rhonda has misunderstood her. She recognises the ambiguity in the situation (which of the two charts is being referred to) and resolves it by asking questions. She also recognises that her teacher has made incorrect assumptions and adapts the questions she asks Rhonda to ensure that she gets the information she needs. Teacher and child collaborate in establishing that they are both looking at, talking about and acting on the same part of the same chart.

When we look at Hannelore's progress during the year it seems that she had developed a number of different understandings and competences simultaneously: she developed some control over the production of written language; an awareness of the latent ambiguity of language; an appreciation of the need for precision in the expression of meaning; an active consideration of how others might interpret what is said or written; and growth in conversational competence. We are not speculating about causal relationships between these different strands of development but it is clear that the outcome for the children involved in Rhonda's literacy programme was more complex and richer than it would have been had Rhonda tried to direct and control each child's learning as they progressed through a prescriptive and highly structured programme of literacy instruction. Hannelore has not just learnt to write. She has also become a better thinker and communicator.

The notion that 'lower order skills' must be brought to a level of automaticity before interpretation and the attribution of meaning can be dealt with takes no account of what is perfectly clear: that one form of development does not occur in isolation from others. As we learn one thing we make connections with other things which are not necessarily obviously related to the primary thing we are learning. And development in one area inevitably influences our competence in other areas. So learning to write enhances the ability of children to deal with ambiguity in language, and to think about other how other people might interpret what they say and write. Growth in these areas will in turn influence the children's competence as speakers and writers. And that growth in competence will cause further growth in other areas... and so it goes. As Olson (1986, 1996) suggests, even the way children think about the world and construct knowledge might be fundamentally influenced by the development of literacy. Teaching children prescriptively to read and write, and insisting that learning to be literate must require isolated analyses of words and developing automatic responses to print through drills and practices can be counterproductive to what the children learn, but even more to what they fail to learn. We argue that this prescriptive approach might retard, perhaps permanently, not only the growth of a rich and empowering form of literacy but also the development of children's communicative competence and the growth of important understandings of language, other people's minds and the world at large.

Learning More Than Is Taught

Children certainly learn to read in programmes with a heavy emphasis on the direct teaching of grapho-phonemic relationships. Marie Clay (1987) has, with characteristic good sense, observed that while different reading programmes have different emphases, most routes lead to efficient reading for most children. But such good results, she also says, are attributable to the fact that successful learners overcome the short-comings of the instructional programmes in which they are involved, and the limitations of the teachers who deliver them, by actively working on their own reading response systems, just as most children build their own oral language systems. Successful readers do much more than they are being taught to do. They seek to make sense of written language for themselves, rather than being completely depen-dent on instruction, and they '... self-schedule reading training for themselves in those areas neglected by the programme'. By contrast, children who are poor readers, Clay says, do *only* what they are being taught (1987, pp.163-165).

This book examines writing development rather than reading develop-ment. But our observations of five-year-olds learning to write in Rhonda Fisher's classroom suggest that what Marie Clay had to say about successful readers is also true of successful writers. We have focused on Emma and Hannelore because they were successful writers, and noted how they did more than learn to write simple sentences on topics set by the teacher. In the space of a few short months they be-came actively involved in developing their own writing production systems. They chose their own topics, even when the teacher clearly indicated that other topics were more appropriate. They discussed their 'stories' with other children, considering word choices and differing about spelling options. They learnt about words from the reading they did, often surprising their teacher with what they knew and could do. And although they were only five years old and right at the beginning of their development as writers, they sometimes wrote texts which reflected on personal experience rather than just recording it.

It is also true that, during the year, they became progressively less dependent on the support of their teacher. Incidental, independent learning became much more common. In the following episode, for example, Hannelore corrects her spelling because she notices what Rhonda is saying to another child. This extract involves the children who were writing about the Sports Carnival.

Episode 6.4

In her 'story' Hannelore has already written 'sports' twice as 'spoots'. Rhonda does not seem to have noticed this. Emma is also writing 'Yesterday we had a Sports Carnival.' Rhonda looks at Emma's text. She has written

yesterday we had ar spa

Rhonda points at 'spa' in Emma's text. She looks around at the other children at the table as she speaks.

Rhonda: sp * sp * sp * or-tuh

Nobody responds. Rhonda looks around at the children again. She now has their full attention.

Rhonda: or * what's the or?

Emma: A-W

Rhonda: no no not that 'or' ** O/

Emma: U

Rhonda: no * spor * sports * sp * what comes next?

A little earlier Rhonda had helped children at a table on the other side of the room with the spelling of 'sports'. She now turns and speaks to them.

Rhonda: What was that 'or' sound in 'sports'? S-P ** O

Hannelore has been listening. She crosses out the second 'O' in 'spoots' in both places where she has written it and waits.

The children at the other table call out 'R'.

Rhonda: R

Hannelore writes 'r' in place of the letters she has crossed out.

What is happening here resembles the time when one of our colleagues was building a retaining wall. He had decided that he should take on the challenge although he knew that he did not have the requisite skills or experience and had little confidence in himself as a wall builder. To prepare himself for the task he asked questions and gathered advice. Then he started to build the wall and, as he proceeded, something happened. He started to notice the existence of other retaining walls. When he stopped his car to examine them he found that he was looking at them with new appreciation and understanding. He noticed details that would have escaped his attention before he became a novice builder. And as he became more aware of the principles that governed the building of effective retaining walls, he also became better at learning about wall construction just by looking at the walls. When he found someone actually constructing a retaining wall he watched what they were doing with enhanced understanding. He could now look specifically at what good wall builders did to avoid the problems he had encountered. And now, when he asked questions, they were focused exactly on the things he needed to know to help him become not only a better but also a more conventional, wall builder.

This is pretty much what happened to Hannelore in Rhonda's classroom. From January to August, she had become a writer. It is true that she was still a novice but she had become much more aware of the details of written language. She now noticed things that she would have missed when she was less confident and competent. She had developed a written language production system that was incomplete but which nevertheless embodied the principles of written language production. In other words, although she was still a novice writer, she understood a fair amount about the nature of written language.

When in Episode 6.4 Hannelore pauses to listen to the exchange between Emma and Rhonda, her attention is captured by Rhonda's comment about how 'sports' is spelled. Like our colleague whose wall building made him more aware of the structural details of walls, Hannelore's involvement in writing has made her more consciously aware of the structural details of written words. Having actively grappled with the problem of how to write 'sports' herself, she notices what is being said about the conventional spelling of the word. Without any overt sign that she is checking her text (like reading back through what she has written and pointing to the words), she locates the precise part of the word that needs to be corrected and crosses it out. Then she waits for the information she needs in order to correct what she has written. When it is provided she writes 'r' in both words in place of the crossed-out Os. She is listening with full understanding and with a precise attention to detail which can only have come from her own involvement in and understanding of the process of writing. She does not need to have everything explained to her. She does not need repeated drills to develop automaticity of response. She is behaving as a rational being who is capable, when the occasion arises, of generating new understandings for herself about the nature of writing.

This act of learning could not have taken place if Hannelore had been working in isolation or in a classroom in which children were silently writing on set topics under the close supervision of the teacher. She learns how to spell 'sports' because she is part of a community of writers. She is surrounded by other children who are not only writing but who are also talking about what they are doing: asking questions, offering advice, making comments. Rhonda has encouraged this. Her conversations with individual children were *never* isolated exchanges. As she engaged in dialogue with one child she always invited others to offer help and make comments. As a result, it was normal in this class-room to eavesdrop on nearby conversations and make unsolicited contributions to them. In Episode 6.4 Hannelore does not make a contribution to the conversation she hears but she does listen and respond privately. No-one notices what she is doing but she is still clearly involved, if only incidentally, in the talk that is going on, and it is that involvement that permits her to learn something new about writ-ing. Her learning is social in nature but that does not always imply direct involvement in learning conversations. Both Hannelore and Emma often learned from what was happening in the classroom even when they were only onlookers or eavesdroppers.

Conclusion

Marilyn Jagar Adams (1994) has said that, relative to the overall literacy challenge...

> learning to recognise words is a very small component. Yet it is also wholly necessary. In the end, the print on the page constitutes the basic perceptual data of reading. Rather than diverting efforts in search of meaning, the reader's letter- and word-wise processes supply the text-based information on which comprehension depends. As fluent readers move quickly and easily through the print, literal comprehension auto-matically unfolds apace. (Adams, 1994, p.858)

But the aim of reading is rarely literal comprehension, and Adams goes on to say that the full interpretation of a complex text involves the use of prior knowledge, the retrieval from memory of relevant facts and the exercise of the critical and inferential capacities needed to draw together these various sources of information so that proper sense can be made of what has been read. The effort and thought that readers can invest at this level of interpretation of a text depends on '... the ease and completeness with which they have executed the levels that support it' (p.859). That is, the active exercise of attention, the strategic use of memory and complex interpretive processes will only become involved if the 'basic perceptual data' are being received and processed by the reader without conscious effort. The development of automatic responses to the orthological and phonological aspects of print 'enables' skilful reading. You can't become a fluent reader if you haven't first done the hard work on the 'basic' processes.

It is such views which provide the basis for the recommendations for teaching reading made by Roger Beard and Jane Oakhill (1994) in their critique of Liz Waterland's monograph, *Read With Me* referred to in the first chapter. We have chosen to focus on Beard and Oakhill's work partly because it is in its essentials a recent and representative statement of a widely held position. But it is also of interest because it seeks common ground between conflicting approaches to teaching reading. Beard and Oakhill emphasise the importance of enjoyable reading experiences for young children. They advocate frequent reading of carefully chosen books, even after the children can read for themselves. Through such experiences, they say, children can be exposed to 'book language' and enlarge their vocabularies. Their teachers can also engage them in making sense of those stories through questioning and discussion. Beard and Oakhill also suggest that early efforts should be made to develop the children's awareness and enjoyment of rhymes and to teach them about print conventions.

They also try to avoid extremes in their suggestions about the role of phonics in reading instruction. They make it clear, for example, that they are not advocating that '... phonic rules should be taught before children learn to read'. Current evidence, they say, suggests that '... learning to read and becoming aware of the sound system of the language go hand-in-hand'. And they cite research that indicates that beginning readers might not be able to engage in phonemic segmentation and blending. They suggest, therefore, that children might begin reading by being taught a 'small sight vocabulary' so that they can read simple stories, perhaps their own dictated ones. At first, they say, children can be encouraged to use context to guess at words and check if their reading makes sense. But once they know most of the letter sounds, formal analysis of words should begin. At first this might just involve pointing out similarities between words and changing one word to another by changing onset or rime. At this point they make it absolutely clear that, whenever it begins and however it is done, children must be taught strategies for decoding words (pp.29-33). The majority of children, we are told, still learn to read because they are taught, not despite it.

Despite their admirable efforts to find a compromise between what they see as the extremes of Waterland's 'apprenticeship approach' and equally extreme approaches characterised by dull phonic drills, what Beard and Oakhill suggest is still absolutely consistent with the bottom-up information processing view of reading proposed by Adams: that reading consists of complex information processing; that lower level perceptual processing must be brought to automaticity before the reader is able to attend to the meaning of what is written; and that if children are to become independent readers they must be taught decoding stategies so that they will be able to read unfamiliar texts. There is no doubt about their position. They assert more than once that reading is a highly *complex* process and that the vast majority of children must be explicitly *taught* phonological awareness and word decoding skills as prequisites for the development of fluent, independent reading.

As we said early on, one of the impulses for writing this book was our reading of Beard and Oakhill's critique of *Read With Me*. As critiques go, it is civil and conciliatory in tone, reasonable and moderate. But at the same time it provides an indication of the influence exerted by people like Marilyn Jager Adams on teaching practices. We believe that such a view does not adequately explain what successful learners do in actual classrooms as they gain control over reading and writing. And we believe this is important, because understanding successful learning seems to offer the best chance of developing better literacy programmes in our schools. It is not Beard and Oakhill's beliefs about the need for children to master the alphabetic principle or learn grapho-phonemic correspondence rules that matters. It is their beliefs about *how* those things are to be learnt that is significant, and that is what we have been trying to examine in the last six chapters.

We have tried to present a different perspective on literacy development, based on assumptions about learning which are different to those made by Adams and Andrews or by Beard and Oakhill. We have focused on writing rather than reading, because writing is the productive aspect of written language, just as speech is the productive aspect of spoken language. And because it is productive it requires children to put their knowledge of all aspects of written language to the test every time they write. It is not possible to write without using the alphabetic system and coming to grips with the way it works. And it is impossible to communicate in writing without taking meaning into account or without thinking about how potential readers might interpret what has been written. The neglect of writing is the most serious deficiency of Beard and Oakhill's 'more balanced approach'. To us it is the act of writing that provides the best opportunities for learning about the nature of written language. If teachers followed Rhonda Fisher's example and involved children in writing from the very beginning of formal schooling, explicit teaching of phonemic awareness and word decoding would not be needed.

Our account of the literacy learning that went on in Rhonda Fisher's classroom presents literacy as a set of social practices. From our perspective what the children were learning was how to participate in the social activities of their classroom. The learning we observed is probably best described in Barbara Rogoff's terms, as 'transformation of participation'. From this perspective '... learning and development are conceived of as a process in which people transform the roles that they play in the sociocultural activities in which they participate' (Rogoff and Toma, 1997, 474). The children in this class participated in writing as a sociocultural activity. At the beginning their participation was minimal. Even so, it required a great deal of support from the teacher to keep them involved. As time passed the children took responsibility for more and more of their learning and the teacher allowed control to pass to them. As the children took more responsibility, the teacher took less. At the same time the teacher asked less questions about matters such as which word came next or where a specific word might be found, and asked more questions like 'Does that make sense?' and 'What's going to happen next in your story?' The children's role gradually changed from scribe to author and the teacher's role changed from tutor to editor.

Our account of literacy development is based on a different body of research into learning, much of it concerned with the relationship between instruction and learning. Although this research was often based on adult-child dyads, it nevertheless reflected what actually happened in Rhonda's classroom in a situation involving one adult and many children. Like the effective instructors in the research referred to, Rhonda responded contingently to the children, intervening more directly when the children seemed not to understand but withdrawing when they seemed able to go on independently. She also involved them in shared thinking and joint decision-making, behaviours which research suggests contribute positively to the effectiveness of children's learning.

The notion that children must be taught in order to learn implies adult-driven instruction. Rhonda's classroom, however, most closely resembled what Rogoff (1996, 1997) has called a 'community of learners' in which all the participants work together, with everyone serving as a resource for everyone else. Children and adults collaborate in the learning activities of the classroom and, though adults often guide the process of learning, the children gradually become proficient in the management of their own learning. In such situations the classroom talk is often conversational, and learning consists of negotiations of understanding. Knowledge is not transmitted from one person to another but is jointly constructed. Neither is all learning dependent upon the direct intervention of the teacher. In many of the episodes we discussed we saw the children talking freely to each other about what they were doing and offering assistance to one another. The development of this 'community of learners' took time to develop, but six months after these children first entered school it was clear that they had already formed such a community. In addition to learning to read and write, they were also developing an understanding that learning is something we do together. The experience of being part of such a group seems to have had an influence not only on the development of their competence as writers but also upon their growth into confident and independent learners.

The context in which the children learnt was also significant. We found most useful the definition of context as a mental phenomenon given by Edwards and Mercer (1987. pp.160-161). Context, according to this definition, is intersubjective. It is the common knowledge shared by the participants invoked by the discourse. And it was the changes in context which developed over time (what Edwards and Mercer call 'continuity') which indicated what had been learnt. As, for example, the children mastered the activity structure of writing or ceased to refer to the alphabet chart to match sounds to letters, it was no longer necessary to invoke the activity structure or the alphabet chart as contextual. The letter-sound correspondences and the steps involved in 'writing a story' became part of what was mutually known and taken-for-granted. These things could be acknowledged as learnt. They then formed part of the presupposed knowledge upon which understanding of, and control over, writing could be expanded and elaborated.

Another aspect of Rhonda's role as instructor was, especially in the early months, acting as 'consciousness for two'. She helped the children to attend to what was significant and to remember what was relevant to the solution of the problems at hand. She would prompt the children to remember where they had previously seen a particular word, or an occasion when a specific spelling generalisation had been discussed. She would help the children to keep their place in what they were writing and to remember what their intended message was. And she would break the task into simpler sub-tasks to make the achievement of the objective easier. Another indication of learning was the growth in the children's capacity to take Rhonda's ways of supporting their learning and use them in relation to themselves to gain voluntary control over their mental processes. We knew the children were learning when they no longer needed Rhonda to remind them where a word could be found or that there was something special about the way 'ghost' was spelled. They had made progress in the development of control over their attention or memory or capacity to plan. They had made progress in managing their own learning.

Because the learning the children did in Rhonda's classroom was embedded in ongoing and goal-oriented activity, the children seemed to learn more than just how to write. In producing a 'story' they had, for example, to ask themselves whether their text would make sense to a potential reader, and thus found themselves confronted by the latent ambiguity of language. This meant that a significant step had been taken in the type of thinking done by the children. They were now being asked to consider the operation of other people's minds. And because Rhonda constantly asked them to check what they had written, they were also beginning to learn that the meaning of something can be checked against written language texts as well as against the world. They were also involved, in an elementary way, in narrative thinking; considering what might happen next in their fictional accounts, and choosing what to include and what to leave out of their recounts of personal experience. Instead of being involved just in the ineluctable flux of living, the children were beginning to learn to make experience concrete in writing; to freeze the flow of experience so that it could be examined. They were learning to impose order and structure on what had already happened through acts of reconstruction and choice. They were being introduced to narrative thought; to the consideration of possible worlds and 'what if' thinking. Surely such experiences should not be optional extras in literacy programmes.

Debates about the development of literacy continue to focus on teaching. The matter of central interest in such debates is which 'method' provides the most effective way of teaching children to read and write. We prefer to emphasise learning rather than teaching. We have not devalued the role of the adult in learning but show that the critical features of effective instruction are response and collaboration rather than control and exposition. But our account of the development of writing has not just been about what the teacher must do to produce literate children. It has been concerned with what teachers and children do *together* that leads to effective learning and the creation of active, efficient, independent learners. Contrary to Beard and Oakhill's assertion that most children need to be *taught* to be literate, we maintain that the teacher's task is to engage the children in genuinely collaborative acts of *learning* and to draw them into becoming participants in a community of learners. The episodes we have discussed show that this is what happened in Rhonda Fisher's classroom.

The basic aim in any literacy programme is to teach the children to read and write. But we agree with Marie Clay when she says that most programmes of literacy instruction, whatever their emphasis, will teach most of the children involved to be literate. A more basic aim should be to produce learners who, like the sucessful readers Marie Clay referred to, learn more than they are being taught. The instructional practices teachers employ are critical in this respect because the way children are taught tells them what types of learners we think they are, and children tend to accept such judgements without question. Children who believe that they must be taught in order to learn are likely to become dependent on instruction and incapable of learning independently the things that their programme neglects. These are the children who are most likely to become the unsuccessful readers Clay describes, who learn only what they are taught. Instructional style might well be an unrecognised factor contributing to reading disability. To do justice to the children we teach, our basic objective has to be the development of children who learn a little more about literacy every time they read and write, because they have been taught to be confident, independent and resourceful participants in a community of learners.

Chapter 7

The social action in a classroom, as in any other social group, is culturally patterned (Green and Meyer, 1991, p.143). What is known and what is done in the culture is not an expression of individuality, but is acquired and constructed in the events and activities of the group. Each classroom has its own particular culture: its ways of doing things, its ways of talking, the knowledge it values and the competence it rewards. None of this culture should have to be inferred by the children. The patterns of social action and the expectations about what each member of the group needs to understand, and produce, and be able to do, should be made explicit by the teacher.

The implicit rules governing the ways language is to be used (who can talk to whom, in what ways and under what circumstances) are a central feature of the culture of the classroom, because learning is an essentially social and communicative process. But in many classrooms teachers exercise almost complete control over the talk that occurs. They can talk when they please and to whom they please. They can talk to the whole class at once, to small groups within the class or with individual pupils. And whenever teachers are involved in talk in the classroom they almost always decide what is going to be talked about, who will do the talking and when they may talk. Teachers decide whose talk is acceptable and whose talk can be ignored or devalued.

In an extensive longitudinal study, Gordon Wells (1981, 1985) gathered samples of talk between children and adults at home and at school. He found that children at school initiate fewer conversations with adults, get fewer turns, ask fewer questions, make fewer requests and express a narrower range of meanings than they do in their conversations with adults at home. Furthermore, at school the teacher produces three utterances for every one by the child, while at home the conversations with adults are much more evenly balanced. The syntactic complexity of children's utterances was also greater at home, suggesting that they use their full linguistic resources less frequently when talking to their teachers. The picture that emerges from this, and other similar research (e.g. Tizard and Hughes, 1984), is of children answering teachers' questions and complying with their requests, and of teachers choosing topics and allocating conversational turns.

These findings have been widely accepted as providing a true picture of classroom talk. In fact it is often said that these features of talk in educational settings simply result from the fact that each teacher is charged with the responsibility of educating groups of twenty to thirty children. Teachers dominate talk in classrooms, it is said, because of the necessity of maintaining control and because school talk is directed towards pedagogic outcomes. In the classrooms we observed, however, talk was not as limited in scope nor as teacher-dominated as the above research suggests. We have already shown that Rhonda Fisher regularly engaged the children in her class of five-year-olds in genuine dialogue and that the patterns of language use in the class seemed to make the negotiation of meaning through conversation a common occurrence. In this chapter we will look at some aspects of talk in a class of nine-year-olds.

A Communicative Framework for Learning

Hazel Brown worked with Brian Cambourne on research projects for a number of years. She is widely recognised as an outstanding teacher. Here is a brief description of the way she organised her language sessions. Each session lasted about two hours in her upper primary classrooms.

• Whole class focus time (15-20 minutes)

It is important that any group has times when everyone is involved in shared experiences and activities. This forms the basis not only for group solidarity but also for collective remembering, something that is important educationally, as we have seen in Rhonda's class. Hazel started each language session with such shared activities. There were times when she read to the children; times when she engaged in joint text constructions; times when she modelled literacy behaviours as she talked about them; and times when she discussed selected texts or drew attention to specific aspects of spelling, writing or reading. The children were invited, lured and coerced into participation in these activities. She also frequently engaged in 'strategic thinking aloud': making the invisible thinking and planning processes opaque so that the children could become conscious of them and use them in their own reading and writing.

• Print walk (15-20 minutes)

Hazel always made sure that the children were thoroughly familiar with the print environment of her classroom. She regularly took them on 'guided tours' of the class, engaging them in reading the print on display and talking about it so that the children would remain conscious of what was old and become aware of what was new. The structure and function of the print was, in every case, as much a part of what was talked about as the words themselves. By such means the children were always fully aware of the ways in which the environment of the classroom could be used as a resource for literacy activities.

• Sustained silent reading (20-30 minutes)

We learn to read by reading, so for half an hour each day the children read self-selected materials. This was a quiet time during which everyone (including all adults present) read silently but, because there was to be a sharing time later, the children had to read with that in mind, taking note of the parts of their texts that they might share.

• Activity time (60 minutes)

During this time the children chose their activities and practised their developing language skills, working on activities individually and in groups. These activities included: writing various types of texts; sharing with others their attempts at reading and writing; teaching and learning from other children; retelling known stories; summarising book plots; sequencing cut-up texts; preparing play and poetry readings; and completing posters and charts on topics related to books.

• Demonstration time (10-15 minutes)

During this part of the session the teacher demonstrated skills and tried to develop understandings, working sometimes with small groups of children and sometimes with the whole class. The focus of attention was usually something that several of the children seemed not to have understood, or some aspect of reading or writing which needed to be discussed so that it could be brought under voluntary control. What was usually involved was a short, focused response to a specific need which had been noticed as the children were busily reading and writing during activity time.

• Sharing time

Sharing was voluntary and responses had to be considerate of the feelings of other people. The children were able to share with the rest of the class the books they had been reading, the drafts of what they were writing, or whatever they felt or thought about the literacy activities in which they had been engaged. The other children listened and responded with comments or questions. The teacher listened, intervening only when it was necessary to keep the sharing focused or when she especially wanted an aspect of the sharing to be remembered.

Why This Framework Changes Classroom Talk

In classrooms that operated in this way, the children, like teachers, get to talk to the whole class on topics of their own choice when they 'share-out' during Sharing Time. They talk in small groups as they collaborate with other children in the creation or interpretation of different types of texts during Activity Time. There are also periods in most literacy sessions when pupils have the opportunity to talk with the teacher individually. But as well as having opportunities to talk, the children also learn the ways of talking that such classrooms offer. The children in Rhonda Fisher's kindergarten knew how to contribute to the routine literacy events of their classroom. So do the children in Hazel Brown's classroom. And though what is being learnt is different because these are older children with different needs and purposes to those of five-year-olds we observed, this teacher is also focusing on communication. She is establishing ways of talking. She is inviting the children to participate in joint decision-making. She is involving them in acts of shared thinking and encouraging them to tap into the collective memories and understandings of everyone present. This is a classroom in which learning is a natural social experience.

Zooming-In: Exploring a one-to-one interaction

The focus of this chapter is on one aspect of the talk in the classrooms we studied: interactions between teachers and individual children. Most of these interactions last less than two minutes. Rarely do they exceed three minutes. At first glance they may seem so brief as to be insignificant, but first impressions can be misleading. It is, in fact, during these few minutes of talk that both teacher and child have their best opportunities to engage in genuine negotiations of meaning. The teacher, by responding contingently to the children, can gain insights into what they know and how they are thinking. And the children not only become aware of the limits of their competence and knowledge but they also develop their competence and fine-tune their knowledge by using the teacher's competence and consciousness to complement their own.

Let's examine one of these brief interactions. It was recorded during one of Hazel Brown's language sessions with a group of fourth graders. In classrooms like this, the language session usually comes first in the day, starting at 9.00 a.m and finishing some two hours later when the bell rings for morning recess. Such sessions are typically divided into the sequence of episodes which we have dealt with above, and which are virtually the same every morning.

This exchange, (which is longer than most, lasting almost three minutes) occurred during the 'Activity Time' part of the session. One of the options that the children in this class had during Activity Time was to plan and produce a 'poster session' (similar to those which occur at professional conferences) about an author whose works they had read and enjoyed and which was called a 'Special Author Project'. Typically these children took ten days to two weeks to get their posters finished before they were displayed and discussed.

The child in this stretch of dialogue, Jenny, has chosen Roald Dahl as her author. She has recently come to this class from another school is not yet really familiar with the routines or activities of the class. She is in the early stages of her project and has been writing quietly at her desk. Hazel is walking around the classroom. She is answering questions and talking to the children about their work. She stops to look at what Jenny has written. Jenny's text is as follows:

> Roald Dahls
> The B.F.G., Fantastic M.r
> fox, The Twits, Charlie and the chocolate factory,
> Charlie and the Great Glass
> ellevator, Danny the champion
> of the woulrld, GoerGes
> marvolous medicene.
> I have read The Twits
> and goerGes marvolous
> medicene
> > This is One of
> > roald dahls charaters
> > Mr.s Twit she had
> > ugly thoughts and
> > got ugly. He driscribes
> > His characters well.

Here is a verbatim record of Hazel and Jenny's discussion

Teacher: What are you working on Jenny?

Jenny: I'm trying to do my special author project. I've written a draft of what I want to do on my Roald Dahl Poster.

Teacher: Read it to me.

Jenny responds and reads her draft. Then she looks up at Hazel.

Teacher: What do you want the people who read your draft to know about Roald Dahl Jenny?

There is a pause of about five seconds.

Jenny: I want them to know about some of the books he's written and that he writes about funny events and describes people like Mrs Pratchett and that he's funny and makes you laugh.

Teacher: Well you've got the list OK but have you told your reader about the events and characters he writes about?

Jenny: Haven't I done it right? What should I do?

Teacher: What do you want to do?

Jenny: What I said before.

Teacher: You said that you'd like to tell your reader about some of the funny situations Roald Dahl writes about and some of the characters in his books, didn't you?

Jenny: Yes.

Teacher: Well tell me about them.

Jenny talks about some of the events and characters from some of the Dahl books that she has read. The teacher listens and nods and smiles.

Teacher: Go and write some of those details down on your draft before you forget them and then ask Melissa to listen to what you've written. See if she thinks it's clear. Ask her to help you think of a heading you might use on that section of the poster, a heading that summarises what you're telling your reader.

Jenny: You mean 'Why I Like Roald Dahl's Books'?

Teacher: Yes.

What's going on here? We could be forgiven for thinking that it's merely the teacher 'checking-up' on Jenny. After all it begins with the kind of question that teachers habitually ask to determine whether a learner is on-task. Furthermore, when reconstructed verbatim, stripped of its historical and non-verbal context, it looks like a typical 'teacher-interrogation' of the child. But there's more to it than that. If we look closely at the exchange, we find that there is an underlying structure which is found in most similar exchanges. The talk in Rhonda's kindergarten was structured in ways that helped the children to learn. The same thing is true of the talk in this fourth grade classroom. Hazel is not just checking up on the child and asking for displays of knowledge and competence. She is using talk to help the child think more effectively about specific aspects of literacy.

The Structure of the Exchange

i) Establishing the learner's intent

The clarification of intent is essential because the successful completion of the task is only possible if the child understands the task and its purposes. So Hazel asks, 'What are you working on Jenny?'

Questions like this are part of the habitual ways of talking in this classroom. The children are constantly asked such questions. They might vary in form and emphasis and all might equally well have been asked in this instance:

> What are you doing?
> What are you trying to do?
> What are you supposed to be doing?

or any number of other variations. Hazel's question is a genuine question. She does not know in advance what Jenny will say. Nor is she asking for a display of knowledge to be evaluated – she is genuinely seeking information. We have already referred to the recognition-production gap; that is, the difference between recognition of the desired outcome and assembling the means to achieve that outcome. As David Wood (1989) has observed, such gaps provide instructional opportunities. The question asked will help Hazel to know if Jenny understands what is expected of her; whether she is clear about the anticipated outcome.

Jenny has seen other children's posters and heard them discussed. She is also familiar with the way things are talked about in this classroom. She says that she is working on a Special Author Project and that she has written a draft of what she wants to do.

ii) Establishing a joint focus of attention

Because Jenny's draft and her statement of intent suggest that she does not really understand what her chosen task requires, Hazel's next step is to try to establish a joint focus of attention. The written text is already on the table between them but asking Jenny to read it aloud makes it clear that it is now the matter of primary interest. It is now taken-for-granted that all subsequent utterances in this exchange refer to it, and that the meaning of those utterances will have to be determined by reference to it. This is essential if mutual understandings are to be reached.

Jenny is apparently satisfied with what she has written. She shows no awareness of the inadequacies of her draft.

iii) Fine-tuning intent

Hazel now asks explicitly about the meanings Jenny wishes to convey in an attempt to draw her attention to the gap between her stated intent and what she has written.

'What do you want the people who read your draft to know about Roald Dahl, Jenny?'

Jenny has shown that she is not aware of the inadequacies of what she has written, so Hazel refers to the text which is on the desk between them. She makes a specific comparison between what is actually in the draft and what Jenny has said she intended to write. She acknowledges what Jenny has done ('Well, you've got the list') but then invites her to reflect on whether she has done what she says she wants to do (' ... but have you *told* your reader about the events and characters he writes about?'). Hazel is responding contingently by becoming more specific in her responses.

Jenny does not understand. She is unaware of the inconsistency that Hazel is trying to draw to her attention. She appears unable to grasp the gap between her spoken statement of intent and the written text she has produced. She interprets Hazel's comment as negative feedback.

'Haven't I done it right?' she asks.

There is, of course, no single 'right' way to do it. Hazel is trying to help Jenny to keep her intention in mind while suitable means to achieve it are found. All Jenny understands, however, is that what she has written is 'wrong' and she wants Hazel to tell her in simple, straightforward terms how to get it 'right'.

'What should I do?'

Hazel will not tell Jenny what to do. She is trying to help the child to discover how she can solve her own problem. But Jenny's confusion is obvious. She does not know what is expected of her, so Hazel uses the strategy most commonly employed to repair communication which is in danger of breaking down. She repeats her earlier question, although in an abbreviated form. But Jenny replies, in effect, 'I've already told you that'. It seems that she is not yet capable of holding her stated objective in mind and comparing it with her text, even with Hazel's assistance. She cannot deal with her problem because she does not understand what the problem is.

Jenny's reply also tells us that she does not regard herself as an independent problem-solver and learner. She does not defend what she has written or ask questions to clarify what Hazel means. She simply accepts that she is 'wrong' and that she needs adult direction if she is to put things right.

iv) Working on the problem

Hazel has tried to get Jenny to fine-tune her statement of intent. She was hoping that Jenny might have said something like, 'All right. So you're saying that I need to write about some of the funny events in the books'. But Jenny did not understand what was being said to her so Hazel responds contingently again, doing something equivalent to placing something on the desk between them and then asking a question about it. She summarises Jenny's statement of intent and then asks her to verify it. This establishes clearly what is commonly known (accepted as given) before going on. The clear re-statement of Jenny's intent and her verification of the accuracy of what has been said means that both Hazel and Jenny have restored mutual understanding. On that basis the conversation can move forward.

Next Hazel helps Jenny by exercising more control over the conversation. She asks her to do something explicit which she knows will almost certainly be within her competence. She asks Jenny to tell her about some of the funny incidents and characters in Dahl's books. In effect what Hazel says is: 'You've said you want to tell your readers about the funny events and people in Roald Dahl's books. All right, first you can tell *me*'. Jenny could not manage the abstract comparison of intent and performance, but she can respond to a straightforward directive ('Tell me about them'). She has read some of the books. She knows about the events in them. Hazel is just asking her to remember that information and put it into words.

Jenny is nine years old but because she is confused and uncertain in this situation, Hazel finds it necessary to do much of the cognitive work for her. She helps to focus Jenny's attention on relevant information which she already holds in her memory. She simplifies the task by breaking it down into sub-tasks. She helps her to attend, and organise and remember just as Rhonda did with her five-year-olds. The strategy works. Jenny tells her about the books.

v) Directing and organising

So far Hazel has focused Jenny's attention on what is relevant to the realisation of her intentions and has helped her to bring relevant information to mind. She now asks Jenny to do something with the information which has been remembered.

First, she says, write down what you've told me before you forget it. She isn't just telling the child how to do something that will help her to produce her poster. She is offering guidance on the strategic use of memory. Jenny, like the five-year-olds we studied, can remember information when she is prompted to do so, but she does not necessarily recall it spontaneously. This is probably true of everyone. Given particular problems we need help in recognising, among all the things we know, those things which are relevant to the solution of the problem at hand. We need someone with more expertise, who can see patterns where we see confusion, to help us to remember what is pertinent and to attend to what is significant. This is what Hazel does for Jenny and it is probable that, like younger children, she too will need to be prompted in similar ways on a number of similar future occasions before she finally masters this activity. She is not lacking in intelligence. She is lacking in experience. She needs more opportunities to work on the production of similar posters and to engage in joint thinking and decision-making with more expert others as she does so. Next, Hazel tells Jenny to check the clarity and accuracy of what she has written by sharing it with another child. She is being encouraged to use the knowledge and competence of other children just as Emma and Hannelore were. Hazel's message is the same as Rhonda's. Problem-solving and learning are best engaged in as social acts which permit the use of the group's consciousness.

Hazel is not giving Jenny step-by-step directions for producing a display poster. Instead, she is helping to focus her attention on the process of poster production so that it can be examined and its structure exposed. Once the structure of the activity is familiar to her, Jenny is much more likely to be able to use it independently in the future.

Thinking and responding

The dialogue between Hazel and Jenny again raises questions about the relationship between instruction and learning. Jenny has little idea of what is involved in the task she has undertaken, presumably because she is a relative newcomer to this classroom. She clearly does not understand that conveying information about her chosen author to her classmates involves more than listing the titles of books and making a few loosely related, general remarks. Hazel is aware of the nature of the difficulty but she also knows that telling Jenny directly what to do will be of little long-term use to her. Instead two objectives have to be realised. The first is to find a way of helping Jenny to use her existing knowledge to find a solution to the immediate problem. The second is to provide Jenny with an experience that will make her a better learner, so that when she next encounters a similar problem, Hazel could say to her, 'Remember what happened when you didn't know what to do about your Roald Dahl poster?' Being able to remember how the problem was solved and being able to cue her own memory as Hazel has cued it for her on this occasion would represent a growth in mental capacity, not just a solution to an immediate problem.

This episode further illustrates the fact that effective teaching is characterised by sensitive response to what the child is currently doing about the problem at hand. In order to respond appropriately, however, teachers must first be able to interpret accurately what they see and hear. Sensitive response presupposes informed observation. Accurate interpretation is based on an understanding of what is being observed so teachers can only respond sensibly to a child who is attempting to write if they truly understand the nature of the writing process.

Teaching is a communicative process. It consists of conversations during which the child fine-tunes existing knowledge by building areas of common understanding with their conversational partner. But since exchanges involving significant assymetries of knowledge are likely to lead to breakdowns in communication, the effective instructor will try to maintain the conversation, constantly adapting responses until a basis for mutual understanding can be found. Once again, response is critical. The adult provides whatever types of support are needed to keep the dialogue going, so that the possibility of learning is kept alive. Here are some of the ways Hazel (and other teachers working like this) respond to children in ways that promote learning. Peter Lloyd (1990) has argued that adults enable dialogue with young children to take place by providing a number of important communicative functions. The categories of response suggested here are loosely based on the communicative functions identified by Lloyd.

Focusing: It is not uncommon for children to misunderstand what is expected of them. In such cases the teacher's first task is to help the children to develop a clear understanding of the anticipated outcome and the means by which the outcome might be reached. A plan of attack is needed even though it might be modified in response to later circumstances.

Reminding: All learners find it difficult at times to recall information relevant to the task at hand. It is not a matter of not holding the information in memory, but of not knowing *which information* they need. Teachers can find themselves, in such cases, providing cues to memory or simply asking the child to tell them about some specific aspect of the topic of communication, just as Hazel instructs Jenny to tell her about humorous incidents in Roald Dahl's books, causing her to bring them into focus so that they could then be written down.

Simplifying: In the exchange above Hazel narrows the scope of potential information about Roald Dahl so as to make the task more manageable for Jenny. In other cases, simplifying might involve interpreting information to make it more understandable, or re-stating something in a simpler or more conventional manner.

Clarifying: If the child's responses are confused or ambiguous, or if the learner is obviously 'off-course' (which is different from 'off-task') the teacher will ask, 'Is this what you're trying to say (or do or write) or is it something else?' This alerts the child to communicative failure. In everyday conversation this happens all the time. If we fail to understand what is said to us we either tell our conversational partner that we do not understand what was said or we ask questions to clarify the specific parts which confused us. The teacher must provide such feedback if communicative competence is to grow. Jenny was clearly 'off-course' and her teacher not only made her aware of it but helped her, through dialogue, to develop a more focused understanding of what she was doing.

Structuring: When they first attempt any task, children are likely to be overwhelmed by its complexities. Teachers help children deal with such difficulties by structuring the task for them and guiding them through it step by step. Hazel has done this by dealing with only one aspect of Jenny's chosen topic. She accepts her limited statement of intent and helps her deal with it first by talking about the books she has read, then by writing the information down and finally by finding a heading for that part of the poster. Thus one part of the project has been dealt with. What was clearly too difficult as a large, complex task will be made manageable for Jenny as a series of well defined, simpler and smaller tasks.

Extending: This is usually the move which teachers make if they are satisfied with children's attempts to state and clarify their intent and then decide to push them on to something new, perhaps by asking, 'What else will you (could you, should you, might you) do?' Jenny was clearly not yet ready for such questions.

Instructing: Although Hazel generally responds to requests for assistance by helping the children to find their own solutions to problems, she sometimes intervenes directly in the children's learning. It is important that teachers should know when to intervene and when to withdraw, but to do this they must, through observation and conversation, recognise 'gaps' in the learner's knowledge or skill base which need to be filled immediately. It might be that specific information must be acquired or particular skills developed before the child can once more take part in the shared solution of problems. In general, however, guided participation rather than direct instruction will be the preferred approach to helping children learn.

Referring: Teachers often send children off to another source of expertise, as the teacher did with Jenny. This is an important strategy for two reasons:

- it makes the child aware that there are multiple sources of information and assistance available in the classroom;

- it emphasises the social nature of learning.

Children who are encouraged to use other members of the class as resources for learning become much more flexible in their problem-solving behaviours. As in Rhonda's classroom, these children are being encouraged to use the group consciousness of the class, and its collective memory, in completing the tasks they have chosen to attempt.

Justifying: One of the characteristic features of classrooms like Hazel's is the teachers' frequent use of requests for justification and/or clarification, as in the brief exchange below.

Teacher: What else could you do?

Learner: I could change the next section so that it talks about characters in the book.

Teacher: Why would you want to do that?

The final question has many possible variations. Some of the following are frequently used in such classrooms:

'What do you mean by that? Help me understand.'
'Go on. Convince me that's a good idea.'
'How can you be sure that's true?'
'Find me some examples in the text to support what you just said.'

Learning to deal with ambiguity seems to be basic to successful learning at school. It is also seems to be related to literate ways of thinking and knowing, so it is important to push children into justification and clarification of what they say and write, and to insist that they ask questions of others which seek confirmation, clarification and justification of things said and written. It is by such means that children can be made conscious of their own mental processes. With consciousness comes control, and with control comes independence.

Conclusion

In a recent essay David Olson and Jerome Bruner (1996) identified four ways of thinking about children's minds. They are

Seeing children as doers

This view holds that human competence consists of '... talents, skills, and abilities rather than knowledge and understanding' (p.16). It is assumed that children can be taught what they do not know by being shown. Learning proceeds by way of an apprenticeship during which the novice learns the skills of the expert through repeated practice.

Seeing children as knowers

This view assumes that '... the child's mind is passive, a receptacle waiting to be filled' (p.18). Learning involves the didactic teaching of facts, principles and rules which are to be learned, remembered and applied. Teaching is directed towards the acquisition of knowledge rather than the development of skills and strategies.

Seeing children as thinkers

According to this view, '... children are not seen merely as ignorant or as empty vessels, but as individuals able to understand, to reason, to make sense, both on their own and through discourse with others'(p.19). Teaching is seen as helping children to understand better through discussion and collaboration. By such means privately held beliefs and ideas are brought into a shared frame of reference.

Seeing children as knowledgeable

This perspective offers '... a way for learners to grasp the distinction between personal knowledge, on the one side, and 'what is taken to be known' by the culture on the other' (p.22). Children are seen as having theories and beliefs that have been 'formed and revised on the basis of evidence'. Teaching is a matter of helping the children to evaluate their beliefs and theories reflectively and collaboratively. One outcome might be that children are themselves induced to think about how they know things.

If we use these categories as a guide, two of these models of children's minds can be seen to have influenced the instruction provided in the classrooms we have discussed. First, by asking children to justify what they said and did, Hazel was clearly operating on the assumption that children have beliefs and theories which can be formed and revised on the basis of evidence. She was pushing children into reflecting on their beliefs and finding evidence to support them. She was asking them to seek for consistency and general principles. She was leading them towards a realisation that other people before them had thought about the problems with which they were grappling and had sometimes arrived at solutions which had stood the test of time. She was taking the first steps towards establishing a cultural framework for learning which, if properly developed, would introduce children not just to 'what is known' generally but which would provide opportunities for 'culture creation', the critical examination and possible re-definition of what is known.

These are lofty aims. At a slightly simpler level it is apparent that both Rhonda and Hazel also thought of the children as thinkers, as '... individuals able to understand, to reason, to make sense, both on their own and through discourse with others'. For these children learning to read and write was neither a matter of learning the skills of the expert through repeated practice nor of applying principles and rules but was, instead, a matter of learning to organise their own learning, remembering, and thinking (Olson and Bruner, 1996). The process of learning involved not drills or rote memorisation but the development of a progressively better understanding of reading and writing, and greater control over the mental processes which permitted them to think more clearly about written language and to use it more effectively.

Olson and Bruner also tell us that 'pedagogy is never innocent'. Each form of pedagogy, they say

> ... implies a conception of learners that may in time be adopted by them as the appropriate way of thinking about themselves, their learning, indeed, their ability to learn. The choice of pedagogy inevitably communicates a conception of the learner. (p.23)

Jenny illustrates the point. She has come from another classroom in which different teaching practices were employed. She expects to be told what to do. Her experiences as a learner in her other class have caused her to think of herself as dependent on the teacher for clues as to whether she is 'right' or 'wrong'. She expects direct instruction and waits to be shown exactly what she should do. Her new teacher, however, has different ideas. She wants Jenny to reflect on what she is doing. She helps her remember and sends her off to collaborate in her learning with other children. What Jenny will learn in this classroom is not just how to complete a Special Author Project but also new ways of thinking and a new attitude to herself as a learner. As in Rhonda's classroom, the teacher regards the children as thinkers who, through instruction of the type we have described, will become better at under-standing and problem-solving rather than simply knowing more facts or becoming more skilled.

This is where all teachers should begin. They should ask, 'Does what I believe about the way children think and learn seem likely to develop the children's confidence in themselves as learners or to develop dependence and reluctance to take risks?' If we as teachers want to produce learners who will actively and independently seek to elaborate and refine their understandings of reading and writing, and who will be capable of learning something new about literacy every time they read or write, we must treat children as rational, thinking creatures who can, with the right support, learn to solve problems for themselves. As we will see in the next chapter this is none the less true when the children learning to write are developmentally delayed.

Chapter 8

Brennan is an eight year old autistic boy in a School for Specific Purposes in New South Wales. Two of his classmates are also autistic. Three have Downs Syndrome. Another has Fragile X – Marker X Syndrome. Another is a multiply handicapped, cerebrally palsied child called Tiffany. Yet another child is not specifically categorised but is nonetheless clearly developmentally delayed. Ruth is their teacher this year.

One of the things the children in Ruth's class do is to learn to write their names and addresses, mainly by copying models provided for them. At first Brennan just copied his name. Today Ruth has written his address. He lives in Rothery Road. He looks at the words on the page.

'No. No.'

Ruth does not understand.

'What's wrong Brennan?'

'It's Tiffany. Tiffany.'

After a while Ruth saw what the problem was. She put Tiffany's name card on the desk next to 'Rothery'. She pointed at each word in turn.

'They're not the same word Brennan. The only thing the same is at the end. Let's look.'

Ruth then compared the two words letter by letter, pointing out where each was different and differently formed. When she had finished Brennan was content. He wrote Rothery without objection and without error and has continued to do so, because Ruth had treated him as a reasonable being whose objections had some basis, and who was able to understand a detailed explanation of where he had made his error.

She had treated him as someone capable of attending to and noticing the features of print which made 'Rothery' different from 'Tiffany'. Children in schools of this type have not always been treated in this way.

The Way We Were

Ruth has been teaching developmentally delayed children for sixteen years. She finds the work fascinating and rewarding and is recognised by her colleagues as an excellent teacher who makes a genuine impact on the lives of the children she cares for and instructs. When she first taught in schools for the developmentally delayed in the early seventies, literacy instruction for such children was almost universally limited to trying to teach them to write their own names and addresses and to recognise social signs like Ladies, Gentlemen, Bus Stop, Danger and bus numbers and destinations. At that time it was accepted in Ruth's school that if the children could learn to recognise about twenty-five key then this would permit them to move around their social world without getting lost, being involved in embarrassing incidents or unduly endangering themselves. Frequent repetition combined with appropriate reinforcement was considered the foundation for helping these children to learn effectively. They were taught to write their names and addresses by tracing over dotted outlines of the words. Word recognition was taught mainly by flash card drills. These methods had limited success. Ruth remembers one of her colleagues at that time coming into the lunch room thoroughly exasperated.

'I've spent twenty minutes showing Terry two flash cards,' she said. 'Then, when I asked him to pick up 'gents' he picked up 'ladies' instead.'

In her first months of teaching in such as school Ruth, frustrated by the children's lack of response to these methods, went to the Principal to ask for advice and expert assistance. She was told, 'You've been employed to teach these children. You're the expert. Just do the best you can.'

For twelve years after this Ruth worked as a school librarian and co-ordinator of a resource centre for teachers. Then she returned to Special Education and has spent the last thirteen years in the one school, working with children of different ages and with a very wide range of disabilities. When she returned she discovered that not much had changed. Tracing over dotted outlines of words and repetitive drills of survival words were still central to the literacy education of the children at this School for Specific Purposes. She was still unconvinced that the methods being used were of much use. Even those children who learnt a limited set of words seemed to depend on initial letters in the words and had difficulty in distinguishing between similar words. She was convinced that something more effective could be done. This chapter is about what she did and some of the children she taught. She makes no startling claims about her ways of teaching, but she does know that it brings better results than the methods she was encouraged to use in 1970 and which are still widely used today. She believes that these children, though they have difficulty in learning, learn in *essentially the same way* as mainstream children. She believes that they are active seekers of meaning in their worlds and that the teacher's role as a 'consciousness for two', directing the children's attention and prompting their memories, is as basic to the learning of these delayed development children as it is to any other child's.

In the Beginning

Ruth first made serious attempts to teach reading and writing to developmentally delayed children when she had a class of relatively able eleven-year-olds some years ago. She started by using an activity derived from Sylvia Ashton-Warner (1980). Every few days she would ask each child for a word they would like to have. She then wrote the word on a card and the child copied it. She regularly checked to see which words each child remembered. If a word was not recognised it was discarded. Commonly used words were discarded after three trials instead of one. Soon some of the children were able to recognise fifteen to twenty words.

Just before Christmas, at the annual Miners' Picnic for the children, Santa Claus brought a present for each child. Ruth used this exciting occasion to introduce something new to the children. The day after the picnic Ruth engaged the children in the joint construction of a blackboard story: 'Santa gave me a present'. The next day she printed the same sentence on a cardboard strip for each child. Ruth read it with them while the children pointed to the words. Then they copied the story into their books.

Next Ruth cut 'present' off the end of the sentence and asked each child, 'Well, what *did* Santa give you?' The answer was added to each child's sentence. (e.g. Santa gave me a *car*). The sentence was read and copied.

In the new year Ruth still had the same group of children so she began to expand their stock of words by varying the basic sentence. She asked, 'Who else gave you presents? What did they bring you?' New sentences were constructed. 'Dad gave me a gun.' 'Mum gave me a necklace'. Next the verbs were varied. A new basic sentence frame was constructed to produce 'I like my car' and 'I like my necklace'. Each child had a name card so the step to 'I like Gregory' was an easy one to take.

Each new word card was kept in an envelope at the back of each child's writing book. By the end of the year most children had acquired sets of thirty to sixty words which they used freely to construct stories which they then copied into their writing books. In the second half of the year Ruth would start writing lessons simply by telling the children to get out their cards and make a story. While the children constructed the stories, Ruth would watch closely, asking each child to read the sentence he or she had constructed to make sure that they understood it. Then they would copy the sentence they had made into their writing books.

These methods are not original. Ruth took ideas from a variety of sources, *The Sounds of Language* (Martin, 1972) and *Breakthrough to Literacy* (Mackay, Thompson and Schaub, 1970) in particular, but she knew of no-one else who was using such instructional strategies in schools for the developmentally delayed. The result was that these children showed that they were capable of constructing written texts of their own, limited though they were by the size of their written language vocabularies.

One of the children in this class was Gregory, who had Downs Syndrome. His speech was difficult to understand so he found it hard to communicate through conversation. Like the rest of the children in the group, he had previously only been asked to trace over word outlines so when he was first placed in this class his ability to copy print was limited. This difficulty was made worse because, like many children with Downs Syndrome, he had trouble holding and manipulating writing implements. His copying was untidy and often hard to read. He recognised only a few words.

By the end of the year he had accumulated a set of sixty cards and used them flexibly to create sentences like the following:

Emma (a classmate) is going on the train with Gregory.

I saw Natalie (his sister) in hospital.

Nanny has a red and white car.

I like eggs and bacon.

This might seem to be a limited achievement but remember that even today most children like Greg are only expected to learn, through practice and drill, a set of twenty five socially useful words. Greg knew sixty words. But much more significant than that, he could use those words to generate a wide variety of messages conceived, constructed and copied voluntarily and independently. What we have is not just a method of teaching literacy but a new way of thinking about children like Greg. In Ruth's eyes Gregory was not a different type of being from mainstream pupils. She believed that he learnt as they did. He was as concerned with making and communicating meaning as they were. And his achievements seem to justify that belief.

What Greg needed was the opportunity to transcend his physical and intellectual limitations by being given strategies and resources for communication which he could use voluntarily to produce written language texts. He could, by year's end, construct and copy sentences that seemed well beyond his capacity early in the year. All his earlier years of instruction had failed to recognise that he was capable of developing at least some control over written language.

Making Changes

The classes Ruth has taught over the years have rarely had more than nine children in them. She has always had a teacher's assistant for at least part of each day, and she is always pleased to have the help of selected volunteers. This might appear to be a high adult-child ratio, but it is needed. Many of the classes have consisted mainly of children who were difficult to manage. Ruth told us that in a recent class she taught, assisted by two other adults, the chief task for some months at the beginning of the year was to keep the children in the classroom and in their seats. Most of us would find such groups of children problematic. But visitors to Ruth's classroom will now usually find the children sitting in their desks, doing their school work like mainstream pupils. Naturally Ruth needs to be much more active than most mainstream teachers, constantly monitoring what the children are doing, and responding to and directing their behaviour moment by moment. The orderly nature of Ruth's classroom has only been achieved by using activities designed to teach the children to act as group members, to share joint attention with the others, to cooperate with the teacher and the other children, and to be engaged in joint thinking about whatever has been singled out as the focus of attention. For example, this could mean that they are engaged not just in drawing but in drawing the same stylised Mickey Mouse face as all the other children, under the direction of the teacher, attending to the specific features of the displayed face and reproducing them in response to verbal instructions.

It is widely acknowledged that most young children cannot attend or remember as well as older children. And the growth in children's capacity to use attention and memory strategically is at least in part learnt rather than being simply a matter of maturation. But the children Ruth teaches are delayed developers. It is probable that, at their best moments, their capacity to attend and remember is less than that of a young mainstream pupil. Special and deliberate efforts need to be made, therefore, to teach them to direct their attention to what the teacher says is relevant and to follow directions about what is to be done in relation to the object of joint attention. In other words, they have to be able both to attend to the apple rather than the banana on the colouring book page, and then to colour it red rather than yellow.

Ruth used the following activities in her attempts to achieve these objectives.

• Directed Colouring

The children are each given a number of coloured pencils and a picture to be coloured.

The teacher holds up a yellow pencil and says, 'Pick up yellow.'

She makes sure that all the children have picked up a yellow pencil.

The teacher turns to her copy of the picture, attached to the chalkboard. 'Where's the sun?' she asks the children, putting her pencil on the sun in the picture. 'Put your pencil on the sun.'

'Colour the sun yellow.' And she colours the sun, providing a point of reference for any child in doubt about what is to be done.

Then, 'Pick up blue.' And so on.

At first just selecting the right coloured pencil and colouring approximately the right area of the page is accepted, but as time goes on Ruth directs their attention to the need to colour inside the outlines. 'Look what I'm doing,' she says. 'I'm colouring inside the lines. So is Amy. Good colouring Amy. You stayed inside the lines.'

Part of what is being learnt here is how to do what is expected in this type of activity. In that respect it is of the same nature as Rhonda's attempts to teach her children how competent writers were expected to behave in her classroom. Eventually some of the children are capable of spontaneously colouring in a picture, keeping within the lines, but that is not the most significant outcome. It is more important that the children are learning to be competent participants in school activities. If that is not learnt, then it is far less likely that anything else, including how to use written language, will be learnt either.

• Directed Drawing

This has much the same structure as Directed Colouring but it moves the children closer to writing. The teacher first tapes a piece of paper to the chalkboard. What is to be drawn will be something with which the children are familiar; for example, a Mickey Mouse face.

'We're going to draw Mickey Mouse's face. Pick up brown.'

She turns to the chalkboard but keeps a constant eye on the children.

'Draw a ball.'

She draws a circle on the paper.

'Now you draw a ball.'

The children attempt to draw a ball.

'Now we'll do the ears,' Ruth says. 'Put your pencil at the top of the big ball.'

And she puts her marker at the appropriate place on the big ball on the paper. She checks to see if the children have followed her instructions accurately.

Then she says, 'Draw a little ball.'

She draws a little ball as she speaks.

'Now you do it.'

The second ear is drawn in the same way.

Then, 'We've got the ears. What else do we need?'

Eyes and nose follow, with Ruth demonstrating and being very specific in her instructions at every step. 'Pick up blue. Put your pencil here. Draw a little ball.' And so on. Then the mouth.

'Pick up red. Put your pencil under the nose. Now down, up.' And she draws the mouth as she speaks.

'Now you do it.'

The children are learning not only to follow directions. How Ruth talks to them about drawing will become the basis upon which they learn about controlling their writing. The standardised ways of talking Ruth uses will be used by the children as they write the letters of the alphabet.

• *Learning the Letter Cues*

It is Ruth's opinion that one of the things her children must be able to do before any progress can be made in teaching them to write, is being able to copy reliably. She has found that they learn little from tracing exercises. Consequently she has developed a set of verbal cues which she uses to guide children in *copying* rather than tracing words. These cues are used whenever the children are asked to write or copy words or numbers as they are, for example, during the daily news sessions.

In this example Ruth is guiding the children in writing the date. She talks about how she writes each letter or number as she writes it on the chalkboard, using the same cues she uses to help the children to draw. It is the 12th of March so the number 12 has to be copied first.

Ruth says, 'First one. Stick.' And she makes the stick, top to bottom as she speaks. 'Now you do it. One. Stick.'

'Next two. Fat tummy (she makes the curve) and across (she completes the number with the straight line, left to right at the bottom of the curve.) 'Now you do it. Fat tummy, across.'

Next comes March.

'All right. Now M. Stick (she makes a vertical stroke, top to bottom). Go to the top (she puts her stick of chalk at the top of the vertical line). Down, up, down. (she completes the M making the lines as she speaks). Now you do it.

She guides the children as they write M. 'Stick. Go to the top. Down, up, down.'

And so it goes, letter by letter.

a: Ball with a stick on its back

r: Stick with a hook

c: Nearly a ball

h: Stick. Go to the middle. Hook.

Ruth has discovered that, as the children learn to use these verbal cues, they can control their own writing behaviour and can copy confidently rather than being restricted to tracing. This is not enough in itself, but it is one more step towards giving these children some control over their literate behaviours.

• Identifying Social Print

Although Ruth was not happy with the ways in which the children were being taught to recognise key words and phrases in the world around them, she agrees that the recognition of signs in the world is an essential part of the educational programme for developmentally delayed children. They might not become fully literate but they must be able to recognise those signs which will permit them to function independently in their social world.

Like many teachers in such schools, Ruth takes the children in her class on excursions: to the dentist's surgery; to the butcher; to the hairdresser. Sometimes they catch trains and buses and go to shopping centres. As they go, Ruth and her asssistants point to signs and talk about them. Entrance. Exit. Ladies. Gents. Bus Stop.

When they return to school, instead of tracing over the words, Ruth actively involves them in looking closely at the words. Let's take EXIT as an example. Ruth provides the children with the four letters in the word on small cards, and an alphabet chart.

> She says, 'Pick up the one like a comb. That says E. Let's find it on the letter board.'

> They sing the alphabet as they point to the letters until they come to E. They place the letter card over the letter on the board. Then Ruth moves on to the X and the I and the T. She uses the standard verbal cues to identify them. X (cross). I (stick). T (stick and across).

> Next she says, 'Now we're going to make a word out of those letters. If they're in the right order they'll say exit, the sign above the door.'

> She constructs the word with them.

> 'Pick up E. Put it on the table next to your tummy. Now, what do you think comes next? X. Pick it up. Put it next to the E. No. *After* the E.'

> And so on. When the word is complete they copy it, guided by the usual verbal cues. This routine is followed a number of times until the children seem confidently able to recognise and name the individual letters and the whole word.

> Then ENTRY is treated in the same way.

By showing them how to attend to the words the children learn to distinguish between them. They learn to focus on the component letters so that they can distinguish between EXIT and ENTRY even though they begin with the same letter. What they are learning is not a conditioned response to a particular set of features arranged in a specific way, but how to attend consciously and deliberately to the components of words so that they can reliably distinguish between them. They are learning a strategy which they can employ actively in making sense of print.

• *Reading and Listening to Stories*
Ruth uses reading activities as well. The children listen to stories. They watch television productions like the BBC's *Words and Pictures,* which tell engaging stories but also focus attention on print.

The school librarian reads them a Big Book once a week. She points to the illustrations to show how they match the text. She encourages participation. With *The Bad-Tempered Ladybird*, the children snarl 'Wanta fight?' They chant along with the rhyme in *Wombat Stew*. Through such experiences, books and stories become pleasant aspects of the children's lives. Reading is seen to be fun.

And then the children have individual reading sessions. The books currently being used have a picture on each right hand page and a simple text on each left hand page. Meaning has to be established first. The children have to know what the text says so that success is guaranteed.

'What's it going to say? What's happening in the picture?'

Then the adult says, 'Mum is washing the dishes'.

A basic objective is to have the children make a voice-print match, so the adult says, 'Put your finger on the first word. Let's read, 'Mum is washing the dishes'.

And they 'read' with the adult, who watches carefully to see that the pointing is accurate.

'Now. Turn the page.'

And so it goes.

These sessions have a number of purposes. Most important is that, through their successful engagement with print, the children feel comfortable and confident when they handle books. 'Book reading' also helps them to become aware of the relationship between spoken and written language, and familiar with the conventions of print.

• Blackboard Stories

Ruth's blackboard story sessions much like Rhonda's. The topic of the story is always something of interest to the children and is generally school-centred. One recent story was 'Dance Day is coming'. It is brief and simple and related to an eagerly awaited event. Ruth has included 'coming' because it is a commonly used word which might be of use in subsequent stories.

The story is written with a thick black pen on a sheet of computer paper identical to the children's sheets. The 'story' is stated in full and then written by word and letter by letter with frequent re-readings of the text.

> First Ruth says, 'We are going to write 'Dance Day is coming'. What's the first word?'
>
> Only four of the children are capable of really participating in the joint construction. They identify the first word for Ruth.
>
> Then Ruth says, 'How does duh- ance start?'
>
> The children call out duh. Ruth says, 'Duh. D.' And she writes the letter on the sheet, giving the cues as she writes. 'Stick. Go to the top. Out. Back.' The children write with her or after she has finished. When those children capable of copying have finished the letter, she moves on to the next letter and so on through the text.

These joint constructions take place three times a week and the resulting texts are put on display in the classroom.

Moving On

With each year, Ruth's knowledge of literacy development among developmentally delayed learners grows. The children in her current class are younger and less able than those in Gregory's group, but she has followed much the same practices. They do, however, present other challenges. For example, most of them reply to questions with single words or, if their speech is occasionally more elaborate, it is rarely conventional in form. So a fair amount of Ruth's energy in the first part of this year has been devoted to developing their oral language, not just because this is important in itself but also because it is a prerequisite for learning to write.

To achieve this objective Ruth has introduced a new routine into her class this year. Each day she supervises the children while they eat their morning tea and lunch. She has used these occasions to help the children learn about different types of food, the way the day is ordered, the routines of life and, above all, about language. At first Ruth began by asking each child what they were eating or drinking. Brennan would typically reply with a single word. 'Sandwich', he might say. But whether or not he replied, Ruth then played and sang a song about Brennan's lunch.

> Brennan is eating a sandwich, a sandwich, a sandwich,
> Brennan is eating a sandwich for his lunch.

The children learned to sing along with her. And so it went, around the class each day at morning tea and at lunch.

When this had been mastered and the children were replying appropriately to Ruth's queries, she took the next step.

> 'What are you eating Brennan?'
> 'Sandwich.'
> 'What sort of sandwich?'

If there was no answer Ruth provided two options. For example, 'Is it ham or is it cheese?'

The type of sandwich is identified, and the song is sung again, with augmentation.

> Brennan is eating a ham sandwich, a ham sandwich, a ham sandwich,
> Brennan is eating a ham sandwich for his lunch.

The next step was to add the time, because these children have to learn a sense of time and order.

> 'What are you eating Brennan?'
> 'What kind of sandwich?'
> 'When?'

And then, once more, the song.

> Brennan is eating a ham sandwich, a ham sandwich, a ham sandwich,
> Brennan is eating a ham sandwich for his lunch at twelve o'clock.

Now, in the middle of the school year, Ruth can say, 'Frame me a story starting with Brennan', and she will probably get the reply she wants. 'Brennan is eating salt and vinegar chips for morning tea at ten o'clock.' Five of the nine children can do this after six months in this class. It is interesting that, although their normal speech is abbreviated and unconventional, when they sing these simple songs all the parts that are normally missing from their speech fall into place. The control they have developed was evident in a recent session of this type. The children no longer necessarily wait to be asked to frame their sentence. Brennan made his request. 'Play pliano,' he told Ruth. 'Sing. Sing Brennan eating chicken chips.'

Karen

Karen is another child in this class. She has not been specifically categorised but is clearly developmentally delayed. She refuses to speak to
most people or to respond to their speech. But this has not stopped her
from correcting Ruth at times when she has been mistaken about what
day of the week it is.

At the beginning of the year Karen could not write at all. In fact she
had great difficulty in copying her name. As a consequence of her
participation in the activities we have described in this chapter, however, she has shown very marked growth as a writer during the year.
She has now become genuinely interested in print. She frequently goes
to Ruth's file, finds a new work sheet and takes it to her desk to copy
her name and address from it. She has also become one of the most
enthusiastic contributors to group story constructions.

By the middle of the year Karen is able to participate confidently in the
activity of 'writing a story' with Ruth's help. She knows some words
and can find others amongst the classroom print. The following incident comes from a session which took place in June. It is typical of
what was happening during individual writing sessions with Karen at
the time.

> Ruth says, 'All right. You write 'We are going to the shops on Wed-
> nesday'. Start with 'we'.'
>
> Karen writes 'we'.
>
> Ruth cues the next response by saying 'We **are**'.
>
> Karen writes 'r'.
>
> Ruth says, 'We are **going**.'
>
> Karen says, 'I can write that'.
>
> She writes 'gonig'.
>
> Ruth says, 'We are going **to**'.
>
> Karen writes 'to'.
>
> 'Now, we are going to **the**.'
>
> For the first time Karen hesitates. There are copies of the jointly con-
> structed stories on the classroom wall, one of which says, 'We went to
> the shops'.

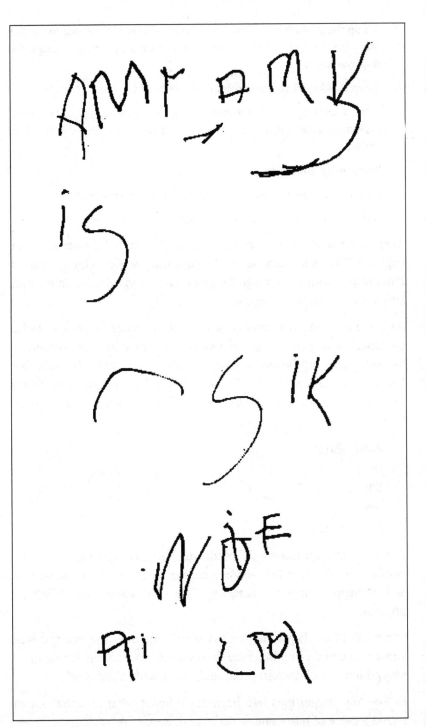

Karen's September text

'It's up there,' Ruth says, indicating with a nod towards the location of the word on the chart. Karen looks. She is clearly searching through the displayed texts.

'Keep looking till you find 'the shops'', Ruth says.

After a few moments Karen focuses on the appropriate text. Her head movement shows that she is scanning left to right across the line. She smiles.

'Now write 'the shops''.

Karen writes the words, copying from the text on the wall.

'We went to the shops on **Wednesday**.'

This time the child initiates the search. She finds 'Wednesday' and copies it. This is no surprise. At the beginning of every day she makes it her responsibility to change the date on the class calendar on the wall and to say the name of the day.

As the end of the year approaches, Karen no longer waits for Ruth's guidance but often rushes ahead. One day in September Ruth nominates the joint story for the day as 'Amy is sick with a cold'. She sees that Karen has already started but lets her go ahead without restraint. At the end of the session Ruth looks to see what she has written. It is as follows:

Amy   Amy
iS
Sik
wif
a   crd.

Karen is now spontaneously producing invented spellings for some words, thus showing that she can engage in phonemic segmentation and phoneme-grapheme matching. She understands the alphabetic principle.

Other things are happening too. A short time after the last text was written, one of the children brought some worms from the school play-ground into the classroom. Ruth said, 'Let's write about that'.

Before any suggestions had been made about what to write, Karen seized a piece of paper and wrote in pink pencil

The
WeMSz

For the first time she has not waited for Ruth to frame the sentence. She has written a sentence beginning or a heading for a story. The incident marks a growth in initiative. Karen is not yet able to frame a sentence in written language without assistance but she wants to be independent. She wants to show that she can do it by herself. She is trying to anticipate what might be said. There is undoubtedly a long way to go before she will be able to choose topics and fashion text on her own, but she is making progress in that direction.

There was a further significant development recently at the end of October. Karen was having difficulty framing a sentence so Ruth started dictating one.

'Today.'

Karen writes 'today' instantly and without assistance.

'I.'

The next two words are 'am going'.

Ruth sounds out 'am'. Karen writes the letters as the sounds are provided. She finds 'going' on a chart and copies it. Next comes 'to have'. Karen writes 'to' instantly. Ruth sounds out 'have'. Karen produces 'hav'.

Ruth tells her, ' 'Have' finishes with 'e'.'

Karen adds the 'e' to 'hav'. Then, without any prompting and without comment, Karen completes the sentence.

Today I   am
going
to   have   a   buf (a bath)

Karen caught Ruth completely by surprise by completing the written sentence spontaneously with a phrase that was not related to her school experience. This was something entirely new. The children have, for some time, been able to complete spoken language sentences when Ruth has provided them with a beginning.

'Frame me a sentence starting with Amy.'

And the child nominated would say, 'Amy is having a meat pie for lunch at twelve o'clock'. But on this occasion Karen has completed a written sentence without prompting. It is a further sign of growth towards independence as a writer. The desire is there. The capacity to write using invented spellings is there. What seems to be needed is an ability to find suitable topics and to frame statements about them in appropriate language forms. Readers will remember that this seemed to be a breakthrough point for Rhonda Fisher's five-year-olds. Perhaps the same thing will be true for Karen. But it would be misleading to see Karen's development as completely comparable with children like Emma and Hannelore. Karen seems to have developed a grasp of the principle that letters 'stand for' sounds and that they can be used to represent spoken words. She has also shown a desire to be independent and to free herself of the need for adult assistance in her writing. What she needs is to develop a greater understanding of what writing is for; what can be written about and how it can be written. That did not seem to be the sequence of development for the younger children. We must take care not to see stages and sequences too readily.

Karen's complete October text

Karen's development as a writer during this year is remarkable, given that she is seriously delayed in development and at the beginning of the year was utterly non-literate. Ruth's activities have not produced such spectacular results with all her children but Karen's progress is enough to demonstrate that it is never sensible to limit children's development by speculating about their potential to learn, especially when that potential is measured by formal tests of mental ability. A year ago no-one would have predicted Karen's current achievements. Who knows what progress the next year will bring? As long as she is given support when she needs it and is allowed to take the initiative when she can, there is every reason to believe that her competence as reader and writer will continue to grow.

Kim

Kim is one of the autistic children in the class and is nine years old. She is a finely built child who, as well as being autistic, suffers from a genetic disorder which has affected her legs so that she moves awk-wardly. Like many autistic children, Kim rarely catches the teacher's eye. She looks past or through people most of the time. She skirts the edges of the room, avoiding passing across the centre if possible.

On a recent trip to the park Sharron, the teacher's assistant, helped Kim use the slide. As she climbed the steps Kim constantly reassured her-self. 'Don't panic,' she said. 'It's okay. It's okay. Don't panic. It's okay.' She had more trouble with the swing. As she was led reluctantly to-wards it, she said softly to herself, 'Nightmare. Nightmare.' Once again we find ourselves wondering about the precise role of language in the experience of such children. It certainly seems to have a part to play in not only the control of behaviour and emotional reponse but also as a commentary on ongoing experience.

In the classroom Kim often wanders around following her own agenda. She goes repeatedly to the window, and then to the bookshelf. She picks up a calendar from the table and examines it, and then goes again to a favourite poster on the wall. She is persistent and it is hard to deflect her from what she wants to do. She speaks quickly and quietly and her voice fades at the end of utterances so it is hard to understand her. She gives the impression of living in an inner world and is easily upset.

During lessons her participation varies. Sometimes she is engrossed in herself and pays little attention to what is happening, but she loves to come out and sing the months of the year or the days of the week as part of the regular morning routine. She calls out answers in group sessions at times, often naming the next letter to be written in the black-board story. Even when she seems not to be attending Ruth will often see that Kim has written the next word in the group story before it has been written on the sheet of paper attached to the chalkboard. This marks an emergence of Kim's ability to participate in group activities, something not characteristic of her behaviour earlier in the year.

Kim learnt to read before she started school by listening repeatedly to a set of Sesame Street story tapes, following the words and pointing to them in the matching books. She persisted with the stories until she could read them. Now she seems able to read most things. She still listens to story tapes and follows the texts as she listens. Her mother says that when she is reading to herself without the tapes and encounters an unfamiliar word she says it softly and pauses, waiting for confirmation that she has read it correctly. She seems to learn most words at her first exposure to them.

When she is asked to read at school, Kim reads with expression but very quickly and her voice fades as she reads, just as it does when she speaks. Ruth has had to teach her to read for an audience. Just as Hannelore, in Chapter Six, had to take into account the possible ways other people might interpret what she was writing, so has Kim had to learn to take other people into account when she reads aloud. Once again we see an example of how learning to be literate has an impact on children's understanding of the social world they inhabit.

Kim can write almost anything that is dictated to her but she does not write spontaneously. Like Karen, she seems not to know what to write – a problem that Rhonda Fisher's five-year-olds had at the beginning of the school year. But Kim's capacity to write is far in advance of Emma's or Hannelore's. Ruth helps Kim to frame sentences, but Kim writes them independently and without difficulty. Knowing how to write is clearly something different from knowing why it is worth doing and what purposes it serves.

Earlier in the year Ruth helped Kim to write about photographs taken on a family holiday. The episode recorded below captures the nature of the talk during such sessions. One photograph was of Kim and her father in the foreground, standing by the edge of a water hole dressed in swimming costumes. Ruth asked, 'What's daddy doing?'

'Rocks. Water.'

Kim's answers are often oblique. She often seems not to answer the questions she is asked. Instead she refers to whatever is of interest to her. This is not conversation. Kim is not responding to what the other person says. In this, as in other aspects of her behaviour, she follows her own agenda. Ruth persists. 'What's Daddy doing?'

'Fishing pole.'

In the background of the photograph a fishing rod could be seen leaning against a tree.

'All right,' said Ruth. 'What can you tell me about the fishing pole?'

Kim said nothing. As usual Ruth offered a choice of responses.

'Is it in the water or on the ground?'

The fishing pole appeared to be standing in the water.

'Ground.'

'Are you sure it's in the ground? Isn't it in the water?'

Kim was insistent.

'Ground. Ground.'

'All right. You write 'The fishing pole was in the ground'. And she did.

Helping Kim to write is not always a straighforward matter. Although she can write most things that are dictated to her, she will only write what is of interest to her and will emphatically refuse to write anything she thinks is not true. And she cannot, as we have seen, frame her own texts. But there are signs of change. The class has been going on excursions to various shops and there are posters in the classroom showing what different types of shops sell. Recently Kim was asked to read part of one of the charts.

'What's that say Kim?'

'Fruit and vegetables.'

'All right. Write a story starting with 'fruit and vegetables'.'

Kim wrote, 'Fruit and vegetables came on a truck'.

It is only a small achievement, but this was the first occasion when Kim wrote anything spontaneously. It clearly grows out of the meal-time sessions when Ruth provided sentence beginnings and asked the children to complete them. But it is also a highly significant step for Kim to take. It moves her a little closer to using writing to record what is happening in her world.

We have kept insisting that learning is social and collaborative. Kim does not communicate as freely as most children do. But one of the interesting things for us is the importance of literacy in Kim's social relationships. Kim has read many Sesame Street books, and this has had some interesting outcomes. For example, one day she was being more resistant than usual about staying at her desk. Ruth would lead her back to her desk and sit her down but almost immediately Kim would be on the move again. After a protracted struggle of wills, Ruth spoke emphatically to her.

'That's enough Kim.'

And she put her back in her chair yet again.

Kim sat in her despised seat talking quietly to herself.

'Enough Grover! Enough.'

Something had been triggered in her reading experience. A point of contact had apparently been made in her mind. She stayed in her seat. We cannot really know why this happened but it looks as though Ruth's 'enough' prompted Kim's memory of an incident in one of her books. And that seems to have led to understanding and compliance.

The effects of messages written expressly for her are shown more clearly in the next incident. Kim likes going camping with her family. One Saturday they were driving through a camping area when Kim became upset and wanted her father to stop the car. Her parents tried to calm her by explaining that they were just going for a drive, but Kim would not be comforted. Finally her mother took out a pen and piece of paper and wrote a message for Kim. 'We're not going camping Kim. We're just going for a drive.' Kim read the note and was content.

Ruth and Sharron use written language in the same way at school. As we said, Kim likes to wander around the room instead of staying at her desk. A few weeks ago Sharron wrote a message for Kim and attached it to her desk. It said, 'Kim. Sit Down. Look at Ruth. Do good work.'

Sharron drew Kim's attention to the sign. 'Look Kim. Read that.' And Kim read it aloud. Since then, whenever she has been restless, one of the adults tells her to read the message on the desk. Her behaviour has changed. She stays at her desk for longer periods and is more attentive. The written word worked where the spoken word had failed.

Kim is certainly a more social child than she was at the beginning of the year. It seems that her experience with written language contributed to this development. As this book is being finished, Kim continues to show signs of change and growth. When Ruth was helping Kim to write about the snails they were observing she was, as usual, prompting her to try to find out what she might have to say about them. The text itself is more orderly than it would have been earlier in the year. It is written in parallel lines in neat (though not well-formed) letters and the page is decorated with oval shapes and a small drawing of a snail at the beginning of one line. The text says

We have a snail in a lid. It has a stripy shell. We have a snail in the bottle.

At this point Ruth asked Kim, 'Where is the snail? Is it in its shell?'

Then she was distracted and turned away. When she looked back Kim had written

Yes in the shell has a snail

This child usually seems to be in a world of her own, refusing to make contact with other people and being apparently indifferent to the intent and purposes of others. She does not engage in conversation. Conversation is by its nature reciprocal, and while Kim usually responds to direct questions and commands, talking to her is a matter of contantly eliciting responses and prompting replies. The replies that do come are incomplete utterances and are often only obliquely related to what has been said to her, as we saw in Ruth's exchanges with Kim about her holiday photographs. In this incident, however, Kim has shown some

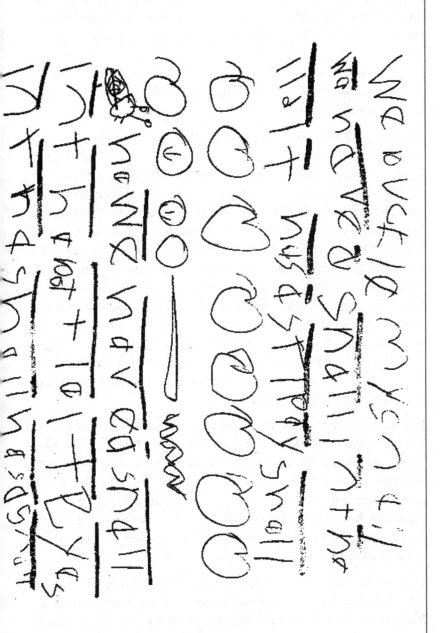

Kim's complete 'Snail' text: November

awareness of the need to make her contributions to a social exchange relevant and sufficient. She has answered a question directly and pertinently, rather than providing one of her customary cryptic and oblique responses. And she has answered in a reasonably complete and well structured sentence. Once again, but in a different way, written language reveals Kim's growth as a social being. This incident represents a first small dialogue in written language with her teacher. It is an exciting development.

Literacy contributes to Kim's life at school in other ways too. For example, it gives her teacher insights into how Kim thinks and what she knows. When mainstream pupils do not understand something they often ask questions. But it is in the act of writing that Kim often reveals what she doesn't know. When she is asked to write a word that isn't in her vocabulary she sometimes becomes distressed, showing her lack of understanding most typically by lowering her head to desk level and making dismissive motions with her arm. The word 'cosmetics' appeared on one of the charts about the shops but when she was asked to write 'We saw cosmetics at the shops', she refused. Ruth suspected that it was because the meaning of the word was unfamiliar to her so she suggested another sentence: 'Lipstick and perfume are cosmetics'. Kim wrote this sentence without delay, presumably because it defined the term for her. It seems that to Kim meaning is of central importance in her use of written language.

Learning to be literate involves more than being able to read and write. It involves learning how to use literacy as a way of thinking; of arriving at new understandings about the world. We saw how Kim responds to worrying experiences by commenting on them, and have also shown how written language can exercise a controlling influence on her behaviour. Recently there have been some signs that the act of writing might also be important in helping her to develop a better understanding of her world, as the following story shows.

One day recently Ruth included the word 'friends' in a sentence for Kim, who not only refused to write the word but was visibly upset. Ruth wrote the word and showed it to Kim, but she still refused to cooperate. She would not write the word. Ruth tried to understand the reasons behind her reactions. Since Kim had refused on other occasions to write words she did not understand, Ruth thought that perhaps Kim did not know what friends were. On the other hand she also knew that Kim did not play with other children at school. Generally she stood against a wall by herself watching the other children and sometimes she retreated to the toilet to escape from the playground. Perhaps she had been upset because she knew she had no friends.

The next day Ruth talked to her about friends. 'Are Amy and Kyrillos friends?' she asked. 'What makes them friends?' There was little in the way of response but Ruth talked on, taking both turns in the conversation whenever she needed to do so. Friends are people you like to be with, she told Kim. They are kind. They make you feel nice. We're your friends. We like to be with you. Dad likes to be with mum. Dad is mum's friend.

> Kim likes the word 'favourite' so Ruth asked, 'Who is your favourite friend?'
>
> 'Adam,' Kim said, naming her little brother.
>
> 'All right. Write my favourite friend is Adam.'

Kim wrote it. Ruth suggested more people who might be friends. There were some names Kim refused to write. She wrote about her parents and then Ruth said, 'Write me a sentence starting with 'My favourite friend is...'. Kim insisted on writing 'fun' despite Ruth's attempts to dissuade her. She was relieved, next, to find that Kim would write, 'Ruth is Kim's friend'. The final text was as follows.

> My favourite friend is Adam.
> Mummy's favourite friend is daddy.
> My favourite friend is fun.
> Ruth is Kim's friend.
> Friends are kind.

As usual, Ruth produced a copy of the story with the class computer and printer. The next day Kim read through all the stories she had written. When she reached the text about friends she read it through and then snatched up a pencil and added the following sentence to her text.

> Sharron is Kim's friend.

This is the first sentence Kim has written which is entirely her own. It is not dictated or prompted. It expresses something *she* wanted to say. The act of writing has made Kim think about what friends are and who they are. Not everyone suggested was included in her text. Clearly she is making decisions about who fits into the category and who is excluded. Most important of all, when she spontaneously wrote 'Sharron is Kim's friend', it is clear that Kim, like any other child, is engaged in thinking about and reflecting on her personal world of experience. Her sentence is about a person who has been kind to her, someone she likes to be with, someone she can now deliberately categorise as a friend. This was the only time Kim elaborated on one of her texts. It seems that her impulse to write might have been driven by a need to make the text complete. If Sharron is not included the story about friends is not finished. As much as anyone else, Kim is concerned with getting the meaning exactly right.

The effects of literacy can be powerful and startling. It is clear that, for Kim, learning to be literate is not predominantly about learning word attack skills or sound-symbol relationships. It is a way of making contact with her world. She can read and write but she seems to have a very limited grasp of the potential uses of reading and writing. This is to be expected – literacy is a set of social practices but Kim is not yet truly a social being. In the above incident, however, there is a clear indication that literacy is starting to play a part in helping her to think about, and make sense of, important aspects of her life. It promises to provide her with a new way of thinking about her world and the people in her life. And these are among the most important things that literacy can do for anyone. They are too often ignored in the literacy programmes offered in schools. They certainly find no mention in information processing explanations of reading development, since such explanations fail to take account of children as beings whose interests and emotions are almost inevitably involved in the reading and writing they do.

Summing Up

The class featured in this chapter is highly significant to our argument. A year ago it was regarded as a difficult group of children in a school where there are no easy classes. They paid attention voluntarily only to videotapes. Their incapacity to attend and remember and their lack of self-discipline made class management extremely difficult. They certainly would not have sat and listened quietly as a book was read to them. Work with such children has its rewards but it is stressful, intense and exhausting.

These children now derive pleasure from books and gain enjoyment from recalling their favourite stories. They listen attentively when a story is read and not only do they often provide correct replies to questions about the books, but the answers are now frequently phrased in book language. They have a better understanding of the detail in books and are more likely to retain what they have heard. In short, even those children who seem to have made little progress in their capacity to write texts of their own have shown noticeable growth in their ability to attend and remember and to use language more effectively. Even in cases where the growth in literacy skills has been limited, these children have nevertheless shown notable and significant cognitive growth. This provides further indication that if initial literacy instruction is too narrow in its scope, opportunities to promote the social and cognitive development in children might be lost.

Conclusion

Many people feel uncomfortable when they step inside the boundaries of classrooms like those discussed in this chapter. What they see are differences: children who look different and behave differently to mainstream pupils. Even school teachers and university lecturers often see them in this light. It is not surprising, then, that many educators have believed that children like the ones in Ruth's class also think and learn in ways that are different to mainstream ways of thinking and learning. One of our aims in this chapter has been to demonstrate that this is not so. Gregory and Kim and Karen and Brennan and all their classmates are in every essential respect like any other child.

It is important that we are not misunderstood about this. These children *are* different in ways that make it more difficult for them to learn, and they need intensive, highly focused and responsive instruction. But learning for such children, while more difficult, is still of the same nature. Like other children, Ruth's pupils are not passively shaped by the world around them. They, too, are actively seeking to make sense of things. They are reasoning about their world and interpreting their experiences. Their interpretation will sometimes be wrong and this can cause behaviour that seems irrational and even bizarre, but when teachers like Ruth begin with the assumption that behind the behaviour there must be a form of reasoning not unlike our own, it becomes possible to find causes and to help the children negotiate better understandings of their world. Ruth did not dismiss Brennan's objections to writing 'Rothery' simply as bizarre behaviour typical of autistic children. She found the reason behind his behaviour and explained to him reasonably why his concerns were misplaced. And he was capable of noticing the differences and, ultimately, of making the necessary distinction between the words.

Learning for these children, as far as Ruth is concerned, is a social process in which she plays an important part. She provides the structure; she helps the children to attend and think and remember. She engages them, to the maximum extent possible, in joint thinking and decision-making. As the research we have cited suggests, Ruth's success as a teacher derives from her behaviour as someone who acts as a 'borrowed consciousness' for her pupils, who leads by following and who involves the children, to the limits of their capability, in the social experience of learning. Just like the five-year-olds we observed in Rhonda's class, these children also gradually found themselves less in need of an adult to do their thinking and remembering for them. As they were able to take control over aspects of their learning, Ruth allowed them to do so.

Ruth and Rhonda have a great deal in common as teachers. They both established predictable, standardised formats for communication within which the children knew exactly what was expected of them. Both teachers worked hard on establishing joint attention. For Rhonda one challenge was to teach the children voluntary control of their memories through the use of language. For Ruth a challenge was to teach the children voluntary control of copying print through the use of language. The term 'developmental delay' is probably apt. It does indeed seem that Ruth's pupils are delayed in development by the difficulties they experience in attending and remembering and planning. But delay in development cannot be taken to imply differences in thinking, and teachers who view developmentally delayed children as Ruth does will enhance their pupils' learning opportunities because they will be treating them as they should be treated: as children who think and learn in essentially the same way as any other child.

Chapter 9

A few years ago Phil Fitzsimmons met Sandra in the local shopping mall. Like him, she'd gone shopping on a wet Sunday afternoon to escape from her kids. Especially from Lucy. 'Phil,' she said, 'she's been driving me crazy! She's been following me around the house all morning complaining that she's got writer's block. I got so frustrated that I threw the Mills and Boon that I'd been reading at her and told her to go and read it. Then I went shopping.'

Does this exemplify Vygotsky's theories in practice? Is this an adult introducing her child to the intellectual life of those around her. It certainly is! We have seen how education involves the development of areas of shared knowledge with the children who learn with us and from us, and not all that knowledge comes from school. The world of the family makes at least as great a contribution as the school to the development of children's knowledge. Shared knowledge, whatever its source, forms the basis of the conversations in which both adult and child fine-tune their understandings of the world around them. And on that wet Sunday, Mills and Boon romance fiction became part of what Lucy knew, as well as being part of what her mother knew and her teachers knew and was, as a result, potentially available as a basis for building knowledge both inside and outside the classroom.

Jerome Bruner (1986) observed that

> a culture is as much a forum for negotiating and renegotiating meaning as it is a set of rules or specifications for action. Indeed, every culture maintains specialised institutions or occasions for intensifying this 'forum-like' feature. Storytelling, theatre, science, even jurisprudence are all techniques for intensifying this function – ways of exploring possible worlds out of the context of immediate need. (p.123)

Reading Mills and Boon involved Lucy in a new way of story telling. She was learning about how those authors tell their stories and about the reality they were creating with their language. Some people might see this as an experience of reading that a girl of Lucy's age could well do without. But Lucy did not receive the information passively and let herself be controlled by it. We know this because she turned up in class the next day and shared with us the writing she'd been doing at home. This is what she wrote:

> Owen's warm breath fanned my rosy cheeks. His words came out with a whoosh. The seams on our jeans were touching. Owen cupped his hand around my chin as he passionately kissed my dry lips. The snow flakes fell upon us. We were interrupted by Emma McRood. Her tight purple mini dress ran perfectly down her perfect figure. Her blond hair danced in the wind like birds flying free. Owen slapped me hard on the back as if to say it's over and walked off with Emma.

In this piece of writing Lucy is engaging in what Bruner calls 'reflective intervention'. She hasn't just absorbed the lurid story lines. She is not being controlled by the knowledge of romance fiction that she has gained from reading the book. She isn't passively accepting the imperatives of a patriarchial society or accepting that the significance of a woman's life is defined by her relationships with men. She has 'penetrated the knowledge for her own uses' and she is capable, as this piece of writing shows, of sharing this with others. By adopting the style and vocabulary of a Mills and Boon novel she shows that she is capable of examining and reflecting on this aspect of her culture, recreating it for her own uses and inhabitating it with her own meanings. It is far too easy to reject such pieces of writing as simple imitation. To imitate well we must be able to do two things. We have to recognise the intent behind what is said or written, and we must understand the choices the speaker or writer makes in realising that intention. All indications are that Lucy has done precisely these things. This is not uncommon. Many parents of children who read extensively find their children passing through phases in their writing which are determined by what they are reading at any particular time, be it the Judy Blum phase, the Sweet Valley High phase or whatever.

This link between reading and writing is important, not just for gifted children like Lucy, but for all children. A well known Australian journalist has succinctly stated his six rules for becoming a good writer as: Read. Read. Read. Write. Write. Write. Those who write fluently and flexibly recognise the value of this advice. But most of us have to be made aware of what comes naturally to only a few. Lucy is instinctively doing what most children need to be encouraged to do – she is reading reflectively. She is thinking, 'That's something different. I wonder how she did that?' and then trying it for herself. She is giving herself practice at being a Mills and Boon author. This does not mean that she will be fixed in that style for the rest of her life. What it does mean is that she can use it when she wants to. It has become part of her repertoire.

One of the things your authors sometimes do with our university students is to give them brief prose passages taken from various types of books: detective stories, romantic fiction, newspaper articles and interview transcripts among others. The passages are carefully chosen so that the type of text they are drawn from is not obviously signalled. We have found that, given these brief extracts from books, students are surprisingly good at recognising a range of styles. Avid readers are better at recognising text types than those who read rarely and reluctantly, but very few of the students – not even those who read widely – seem to do what Lucy has done. Children like Lucy should be of particular interest to those interested in education because they show us what effective learners do. From what comes naturally to Lucy we might be able to extract circumstances and practices that might help other less precocious learners to do something similar.

How Did It Happen?

Lucy learned to read and write before she came to school. Yet, interestingly, she has very few memories of reading and writing in her first three years of school. On the other hand her memories of reading and writing at home in the same period are vivid. And she has no doubt about where her ideas for writing came from. She told us herself:

> Mum and dad always read to us. That's where my ideas came from, to start with anyway. I guess I still do use books most of the time. We'd talk about my writing as well. I learned to spell by reading at home and asking them.

Lucy's parents, Sandra and Bob, were intelligent, energetic people who were doing all they could to encourage their children to do well at school but they were not academics or school teachers. They were both business people who had come from a small, conservative, rural town. They wanted to make sure that their children's development would not be limited by conservatism as theirs had been.

Both worked at home. Every evening they did paper-work in the family room, in the company of their children. When Sandra wasn't attending to business matters she wrote to her twelve overseas pen-friends. Both parents talked to their children and read to them. They never had time to watch television. From an early age Lucy joined them at the living room table. Her first efforts were simple squiggles, circles and lines, but after a while she began to ask how to write words. Her parents would simply write down the words requested on a piece of paper and Lucy would copy them onto her own page.

Sandra and Bob read to Lucy every day, and as they read they asked her questions about what was being read. They would invite her to predict what was going to happen in the story, about who was doing what and to whom. And they talked about the illustrations: 'Who's that? What's he doing?' and so on. Soon Lucy began to ask questions of her own. She pointed to words and letters and asked 'What word is that?' and 'What does that say?'

Sandra and Bob answered her questions. They told her the words. They named the letters. And when she wrote they helped her spell the words she wanted. But as time went on and Lucy became more competent Bob told us that the pattern of dialogue changed.

> She'd ask a question and then give her own response. The questions changed from wanting direct responses and exact things to more of a clarification that she was right, I suppose.

What Bob has to say sounds very much like other accounts of children learning to be literate before school. The child takes the lead. She tries to use what she already knows about print to write a story. As her text develops, she turns to adults to get their response to what she has done and to help her with any difficulties. Just as the children in Rhonda's class gradually appropriated her ways of questioning to guide them-

selves through the process of writing their 'stories', so did Lucy appropriate the model her parents provided for her. Here is yet another small
piece of evidence to support the claim that an essential part of becoming an effective problem-solver is to learn how to cue the recall of relevant items from memory. Lucy does it by asking questions which she
answers herself – answers which must have come from her memories
of earlier attempts to write and earlier similar conversations with her
parents. In time she no longer needed actually to ask the questions.

Her father, Bob, notes changes in Lucy's questioning which reflect the
development of her control over writing. Lucy comments on *other*
changes that took place. For example, she says

> I used to ask mum and dad how to spell words when I was little, but I'm
> not sure. I think I stopped after a while. I took over.

She took control. And, like all good teachers, Lucy's parents let it
happen. When she wanted to try something by herself, they didn't get
in the way. They just waited until they were needed, until she asked the
next question.

As Lucy became more competent as a writer the information she asked
for altered. She no longer needed specific information, such as how to
spell a certain word. Instead she needed to be told whether her attempts
to solve the problems she was having in shaping her plots and refining
her meanings were satisfactory. This matches the behaviour we noted
in the five-year-old beginning writers in Rhonda's class who turned to
her constantly for confirmation as they wrote their texts until they were
confident enough to proceed by themselves. Lucy was concerned with
solving different types of problems, but our observations suggest that
the behaviour of the learner remains remarkably consistent across
settings and across the ages of the children involved. We all need someone to answer our questions and to reassure us that we're doing things
correctly.

None of this differs from the nature of learning in our adult lives.
Perhaps we are making our first apple pie and it just doesn't look the
way it should. If, like Lucy, we are fairly sure of what we need to know,
fortunate enough to have an expert nearby and sensible enough to ask
a question or two, we should be able to produce a pie fit to eat and

pleasing to the eye. And in the process we will have begun to learn something. 'Begun' because it is likely that we will need to seek help more than once before we can remember precisely what we need to know to make outstandingly good apple pies. Like Lucy we will reach a stage when we turn to the expert pie maker and ask, 'Is that right? Is that the way to do it? Should it look like that?' Eventually we will have new questions to ask before we can make other pies requiring different types of pastry or different varieties of filling. But if pie-making is a purpose that matters to us, we will probably persist so that eventually we will become self-regulating pie-makers, able to deal with the ambiguity and confusion that arise as we engage in each new act of pie-making, and capable of demonstrating our pie-making competence whenever the occasion requires us to do so.

Lucy's story also shows us how important it is that we recognise the importance of affective influences on learning. Sandra and Bob weren't focused exclusively on literacy in their interactions with their children. They encouraged Lucy and her brother to be outspoken and confident – to explore possibilities and test assertions. This had a discernible impact. Lucy's willingness to make her views known made her conspicuous at school. But her parents still encouraged her to speak her mind. They wanted her to be independent in action and thought, and in what she wrote. Bob said that before Lucy went to school he and his wife

> just encouraged her to write. She would come and show us what she'd done and we'd praise her. She'd often re-write a story and put in her own comments or add detail.

When Lucy went to school her parents continued to read to her on a nightly basis, but her growth as a reader and writer continued to accelerate. Lucy not only kept searching for new themes and story lines, she also 'wanted her stories to sound right and be more real' and kept coming to her parents for advice and assistance. In response to these approaches, and because they weren't sure how to help her, Sandra and Bob asked Lucy to write a synopsis for each new story. Armed with her ideas Lucy would then approach her parents to elicit their response to what she proposed to write. While they remained supportive, their expectations had risen and they required Lucy to justify her decisions and to explain herself clearly. Lucy has said that during these discussions

> Mum and dad were very honest. They wouldn't just say they liked it when they didn't. We'd sometimes argue ... well not really argue. Sometimes they helped me make it make sense. We'd talk about the books that they had read to me and what had happened in them. You know, characters, plots. Sometimes I'd ignore them if I really liked what I'd written.

After these discussions Lucy would continue her writing. Sometimes she altered her text in accordance with what her parents had said and sometimes she didn't. As Bob also remarked, in the early stages they were a resource that Lucy could use, just as what she was reading and what she was experiencing were resources. But Lucy was unusually fortunate in having constant access to adults who helped her not just to make what she was writing clear but also to relate one story to another, one world of the imagination to the next, one possible world to an alternative one. Ted Hughes (1976) observed that children take possession of stories as units of the imagination. Once the story is well known, it can be re-entered at will and re-examined. The story of the Nativity or the crucifixion or of Lazarus, for example, opens up the entire story of Christ and makes it available for examination and reflection. In this, Hughes sees the beginnings of imaginative and mental control (pp.80-84). Hughes suggests that imagination is not something innate and immutable. It can be strengthened and trained and it is important that this should be done, because those who lack imagination are inflexible and potentially dangerous. Where others see alternative courses, Hughes says, the unimaginative see only a gulf (1976, p.84).

Lucy's parents responded to her requests for assistance in ways that helped to strengthen her capacity to think creatively. When she discussed her writing problems with them, they helped her to re-enter and re-examine the stories she had read in order to see what the authors had done to make their stories interesting and effective. They helped her to consider possibilities and alternatives. This is the essence of narrative and the basis for imaginative thought.

Before the imagination can become an effective tool of thought, however, it must be subject to voluntary control. Vygotsky has said that the development of consciousness involves awareness of the activity of our minds. Becoming conscious of our mental operations and '...viewing each as a process of a certain kind – such as remembering and imagining – leads to their mastery' (Vygotsky, 1986, p.171-172). He illustrates his point by talking about tying a knot in a piece of string. When we tie a knot, he says, our awareness is focused on the knot itself, not the action of tying it. It is only when we shift our attention to *how* the knot was tied that we become fully aware of the process and can explain it to others. Similarly the stories Lucy had read only became part of her consciousness when her parents asked her to think about them. They helped her to consider *ways of writing stories* rather than just how to write a particular story. They helped her to find pattern and image in what she had read so that she could then use the insights this gave her to write better stories of her own.

Lucy's parents helped her to strengthen her imagination and to bring it under control. They helped her to develop a narrative mode of thought; a way of thinking that constantly asks, 'what if?' She learnt to think in ways that were different from children who were less fortunate in their conversational partners. But we agree with Hughes that imagination can be trained and that teachers should help *all* children to exercise and strengthen their creative intelligence in exactly the same ways that Lucy's parents helped her.

Although not teachers or academics and although they had not engaged in any formal studies of education, Lucy's parents did theorise about her learning. Bob told us that

> We didn't know what to do really. We figured that she needed to do it herself, but she needed a reference point. She'd bring a story to us and we wouldn't do it for her. We'd talk her through. I remember showing her what I was reading. I can't remember what it was but we looked at the way the words were strung together.

When we consider our various conversations with the parents of the children whose progress is considered in this book, and examine our video records and transcripts of teachers at work in their classrooms, we are impressed by the consistency of what it all suggests about learning. Although learning is clearly an essentially social process, this does not mean that all the learning children do involves interaction with other people. Since the basic impulse in children is, as we have seen, actively to seek pattern and order and meaning in the world they experience, it follows that they do not always need other people to impel them into such explorations. What we observed Kim doing, for example, illustrates this. She not only initiated and structured her own learning but also chose what she wanted to learn. Her parents only gradually realised what she was doing and then they supported her as best they could in her endeavours. Lucy, too, initiated her explorations of how to convey meaning through written language and chose what she would write about and how.

However, all learning is social, just as the human world is social. Problems will be encountered and the questing child will turn to someone else for help in finding a way of moving on. When Lucy came to something she couldn't do, she says she went to her parents. 'I'd ask and they'd show me or talk me through it.' Children need to have available to them people who are capable of not only answering their questions but helping them to think about what they are learning. In the passage above Bob tells us that he didn't just talk about story lines with Lucy but that he also helped her to think about the ways stories are written. Naturally, he did not generalise about the narrative genre, nor did he try to tell Lucy that stories must conform to a specifically defined structure. But he did make her aware that books were a source of information about ways of writing as well as of ideas about what to write. In various ways each of the teachers and parents mentioned in this book saw themselves in the same way: as agents for securing that the children's attention could be focused on specific aspects of written language so that these aspects might themselves become the object of thought and the subject of discussion.

Although Bob says he didn't know what to do, it seems to us that he had assessed things rather well. Lucy needed a reference point, as does every child. Edwards and Mercer (1989) have suggested that education involves collective remembering, the social construction of knowledge and the conventionalisation of experience. 'Children,' they write, 'do not just happen to reinvent the knowledge of centuries.' The knowledge children develop through their personal investigation of the world needs to be reconstructed, through discussion, into conventional forms so that their understandings can be expressed in ways that others will understand. Then, because there is a shared basis that permits dialogue to take place, children can refine and elaborate their understandings.

It is also interesting that Lucy and her father both say that the problems she had with her writing were dealt with most frequently by 'talking it through'. This fits with how Rhonda responded to children's questions by most often asking other questions. She prompted the children's memories and awakened their consciousness. Lucy's parents were intent not on telling her explicitly what to do but on prompting her memory of relevant stories and inviting her to make connections. Possibilities were opened up for Lucy, but the ultimate decision about how to solve her problems was her own.

Lucy's parents allowed her to shape her own learning. They led by following. They involved her in joint remembering and shared thinking. They prompted the recall of relevant information and stood quietly by, ready to respond when she asked them to, and to prompt her memory and redirect her attention when her attempts to solve her problems faltered. They responded sensitively to what Lucy was actually doing. They did not try to direct and control her learning. Bob expresses it clearly when he says:

> We wanted her to take the lead. And now we tag along behind. We've become sounding boards. We listen and respond but she makes the choice.

This sounds no different from good teaching.

Lucy and Schooled Literacy

In a recent study, Rick Evans (1993) interviewed 65 mainly white, middle class first year college students enrolled at a North American university about their experiences of literacy since early childhood. Most of the students had been above average achievers during their high school years.

Evans discovered that these young people almost all had pleasant memories of their reading and writing experiences before beginning school, and even up until third grade when reading in school was still mainly of stories. But the further they progressed in school the less they liked the reading and writing they were required to do. The teachers had appropriated the activity of reading. They were the ones who understood the meanings of the texts which had to be read. The children's role was to discover what the teacher wanted them to say, and to provide the 'right' answers to the questions the teachers asked.

Evans asserts that one of the clearest indications of the difference between early story reading and reading in the later years of school, was that few of the students could remember the names of more than five books they had read between fourth grade and the end of high school. On the other hand they remembered vividly and with pleasure the names of books that had been read to them, or that they had read for themselves, both inside and outside the classroom in their early years.

Similarly, writing in school was mostly concerned with working out what the teacher expected so that they could get good grades by conforming to those expectations. Writing topics were nearly always assigned by the teacher and mostly required the students to demonstrate their knowledge of certain 'facts'. Writing was valued primarily as a tool for achieving academic success. Evans says that the students understood '... school writing to be formulaic. They accepted that there is a right and a wrong, a correct and an incorrect way to do book reports, essays and research papers'. And they were frustrated when different teachers told them different things about how to present their papers.

These students defined success or failure in terms of the grades their work received. A successful reading or writing experience, they told Evans, was one that earned the highest possible grade for the least effort. Evans hastens to add that these students were not lazy or uncommitted. Their beliefs about reading and writing merely reflected their developing understanding of school reading and writing. Being able to demonstrate that they could do what their teacher required meant that they had to be good readers and writers.

Ironically, the students seldom enjoyed the reading and writing they did at school, whereas outside school they often engaged in personal writing (e.g. journals and diaries) which they enjoyed and valued. They had all enjoyed reading stories and having stories read to them in their early years and they still enjoyed their leisure reading. But much of this reading was regarded as not 'real' reading. Real reading was school-based and was always graded. Evans concludes that

> ... the ways that students learn to engage in school reading and school writing determine their understanding of reading and writing as literate activities generally, and their understanding of themselves as readers and writers.

Thus the students accepted that there are universally acknowledged correct ways to read and write, about which the school knows. Their assessment of themselves as readers and writers depends not on the enjoyment they derive from reading and writing or the usefulness of those activities to them outside school, but on whether they are judged to be reading and writing correctly according to the criteria that schools use to judge their performance. Consequently, reading and writing in schools was generally not liked and they understood reading and writing as '...demonstrations of what they know in the completion of peculiarly irrelevant literate language tasks'. Too often, Evan says, failure in such tasks convinces students that they are not competent as readers and writers – despite evidence of their use and enjoyment of literacy outside the school.

In some respects Lucy's experience was similar, although she makes it clear that she liked her teachers and appreciated their efforts to help her. Her teachers, she said,

> really helped me with my writing ... they encouraged me. But it was stuff like how to spell a word or what kind of word I was using. I had to write what they wanted most of the time. I *wanted* them to show me what they thought good writing was like.

Like Evans' students, Lucy knew what she had to do: to produce what the teachers wanted. But she is also clear about what she wanted and it seems a simple and sensible thing to want. When we set out to make something in the absence of a good model of the finished product to guide us, our task becomes difficult. It is not by accident that cook books are full of photographs of what the dishes look like when they are ready to be served. Lucy wanted much the same thing from her teachers. If they had written with her and shared their writing with her that would have helped. But there were other alternatives. In the same interview she went on to say that

> It wasn't until this year with Mr. Paull that I had something else. He read to us and shared what he thought. He made me do it, all the thinking,

> just like mum and dad. He offered suggestions but I had to decide. He showed us lots of different kinds of writing and talked to us about words; making them *feel* instead of just ... just the right word to use.

What did Mr.Paull do that Lucy found so helpful? He made written language itself the topic of discussion. But he didn't talk about syntax or about standard structures for narratives and recounts and reports. He didn't talk about writing to get through examinations or to earn the highest possible grades. He read the children numerous different kinds of writing – different narratives, different descriptions, different reports – and he talked about what he had read. He showed them what he thought good writing was, and he told them why. He talked about words that not only made sense but which felt right too. He asked the children to make their own judgements about choosing the exact words needed to convey *their* meanings. He helped them understand what it means to be a writer.

Mr. Paull also involved Lucy in joint thinking and shared decision making, just as her parents had done. These are among the characteristics of effective teaching that Barbara Rogoff identified in her research. Mr. Paull also passed control over to the child just as Jerome Bruner and David Wood and Derek Edwards and Neil Mercer have said that good teachers do, whether they are parents or professional educators.

Lucy and the Writing Process

In discussion, Lucy emphasised the influence of her reading on the way she wrote. This was evident in a number of ways. She told us, for example, that she learnt to spell by reading: 'Words just stay in my head'.

Once again it is a matter of memory. If the word is remembered it can be spelled. What we saw of five year-old Emma's and Hannelore's development as writers would seem to support this. Extensive reading seems to be the surest route to conventionally correct spelling. But this is almost incidental to the more important uses of reading that Lucy kept talking about.

> I try to remember what I've read before. I guess I just compare what I've done with what I've read. I do it all the time.

Like most good writers, Lucy constantly re-writes and revises what she has written in the search for a text that says exactly what she wants it to say. This is what she says about revision:

> When I write I'm always re-reading and writing again. You've got all my drafts. I have trouble finishing a story because I always go back. It seems like ... they're never good enough.

At eleven years of age Lucy has discovered what most skilled writers know – that the best thoughts are always second thoughts and that writing consists of an ongoing conversation with yourself. Nancy Mitford, the English novelist, said the following about the way she writes:

> I always rewrite things at least five or six times, maybe more, page by page ... When I sit down to write, the first thing I do is read what I have written the day before, and I rewrite that. This usually gives me a lead into the next thing I am going to do, and it becomes interchangeable with me; the writing and the rewriting. (quoted in Murray, 1975)

Lucy's problem with finishing her writing is familiar to most people who write. As this is being written we are plagued by the same demon: the text is never quite good enough. That it might not be is a risk that has to be taken. Ultimately, if we want to be read, we must finish the text and let it go. The same is true for Lucy and the same purpose will drive her. If her desire to be read by others is great enough she will find her own solutions to the problem.

The difference is that Lucy has already learnt what writing is like by the age of eleven. She knows that many types of have to must be shaped over a series of drafts. She knows that she is writing within a tradition shaped by earlier authors upon whose work she can draw and whose themes and ideas she can vary and elaborate. She knows that often neither form nor meaning are definitively known when she begins to write something new. Most important of all, she knows that although writing might have many purposes (e.g. to keep records, as an aid to memory, to record and transmit oral messages, to meet social obligations through letter writing, to satisfy the demands of school teachers) its most important use is as a way of thinking: as a means of exploring possibilities and considering alternatives. She might not yet know this explicitly, but what she has told us about her writing shows us that she already understands it, even before she has reached secondary school.

Far too many children, probably the majority, never understand the power and potential of writing, or even its most important purposes.

We headed an earlier section of this chapter, 'Where did it come from?' We asked Lucy the same question and she had no doubt:

> It came from mum and dad. Plus just constantly reading. and then writing. I think I compare the ... the things I've read and then write. It just grew and grew.

And a little later she reflects on her primary schooling as she waits to launch into her high school years.

> I really enjoyed school and my teachers were really great but ... I really wish they'd given me the freedom to explore. Just to read and write.

So there it is – Lucy's solution to becoming a really proficient writer and thinker. Read, read, read. Write, write, write. But there is more to it than that, as Lucy herself suggests. You have to keep talking to other people, so that you can establish firmly what you know. Keep talking until you find where what you know connects with what others before you have known. Keep talking until you gain new insights into your problems and can generate possible solutions. Keep talking until you know exactly what you mean. That's what learning is about.

Chapter 10

This book has sought to explore the role played by instruction in learning, and the relationship that exists between beliefs about learning and the teaching practices they engender. The notion that the explicit teaching of grapho-phonemic skills is a pre-requisite for independence in reading is based wholly on research which assumes that reading consists of data-driven information processing and not on the whole picture. It implies a conception of learning as an individual, teacher-directed process and reading as a complex, multi-faceted process in which so many things are happening simultaneously that it is difficult for a learner to do everything at once because of the processing limitations of the human brain. Ways have to be found to overcome these limitations if children are to learn to read. Sally Andrews (1992, pp.88-89) illustrates the point by drawing a parallel between the beginning reader and the beginning pianist:

> In the same way that the beginning pianist must practise low-level skills so that ultimately they can reach the stage of skilled performance where they do not have to pay attention to them, so the beginning reader must practise the low-level skills involved in decoding words and accessing their meaning in order that ultimately they will be able to perform these processes automatically and devote their attention to comprehension.

The messages are clear. Reading is complex. It must be taught. There are lower order skills which have to be mastered before higher order skills can be employed to extract meaning from print. These lower order 'skills' must be repeatedly practised until automaticity of response is reached. Only when specific attention no longer needs to be given to decoding words will attentional resources be available for making sense of the written text. In particular, children have to be explicitly taught decoding strategies so that they will be able to read unfamiliar texts and become truly independent readers.

It seems to us that such assertions about how children learn to be literate are unsatisfactory, not least because they seem not to explain how significant numbers of children learn to read before they come to school. We are not suggesting that such children learn without any adult intervention. But instances of precocious readers provide opportunities to consider how instruction (however defined) contributes to learning. They provide real life examples of how effective learning proceeds, and they have the potential to provide insights into what might be done to help all children to learn with similar ease.

Sam Jordan learnt to read before he went to school. In 1997, when he was six years old, he was visiting relatives with his parents and his older brother Joe. After dinner he was left with Peter, one of the authors of this book, while the others walked down to the river. Sam kept himself amused with pencil and paper on the kitchen table. After a while he called to Peter in the adjoining sitting room.

'Peter,' he said. 'How do you spell cupboard?'

Peter went and looked over Sam's shoulder at what he was writing.

'Let me see what you've written,' he said.

He looked at Sam's sheet of paper. He had written 'cuboard'.

'That's pretty close Sam,' Peter said, 'but you should have a 'p' here.'

Peter pointed at the appropriate place in the word and walked away. A little later Sam collected a number of items he had with him, put them on a shelf in a cupboard and closed the door.

'Do you have any blue-tac Peter?'

Peter didn't, but he and Sam worked out a way of attaching the completed text to the cupboard door. It said: 'All my tings are in this cupboard'.

Peter told Sam's mother, Leslie, about the incident and she told Peter about the way Sam had learned to read. At three years old he was already asking about environmental print. 'What's that say, mummy?' he would ask, pointing to a sign or notice board. Mummy would reply 'Fire Exit' or 'No Dogs' or whatever else the indicated print said. Questions were asked and answers given. There were no attempts at formal instruction.

One day when Sam was about three and a half he was in a supermarket with his mother. As they approached the checkout it was closed and a chain with a message attached was put into place.

'That says 'No Exit',' he told his surprised mother.

Sam had never asked about this sign before. Neither was he just 'reading the environment'. He had remembered words from separate signs and now read them, combined in another way, on yet another sign.

Sam's parents read to him most nights before bedtime. As a baby, he had sat on his mother's knee while she read stories to Joe. Before he was four he would sit on the floor with a favourite book on his lap and try to remember the words of the story as Leslie prepared a meal. Every now and then he would point to a word in the text and ask, 'What does this say?' Generally, once he had been told what a word was, he remembered it.

Leslie knew that Sam had picked up a knowledge of the alphabet because she had found his set of magnetic letters on the refrigerator arranged in alphabetical order. She also knew that he had some awareness of sound-symbol relationships so she played 'I Spy' with him. 'I spy with my little eye something beginning with buh.' Not only could Sam establish, by elimination, the book or the bottle or the banana that his mother had in mind, but he could also take his turn, identifying objects accurately according to their initial phoneme. Sometimes he used this knowledge to help him remember what the print in his books said, so if Leslie was too busy when Sam asked for her help she would tell him, 'You got the last one. Try the next one for yourself. Think about it.'

By four years of age Sam was making clear progress in working out what his books said, but his mother judged that the vocabulary of his *Thomas the Tank Engine* books was too extensive and the sentence structure too complex for him. So she bought two books from the *Ladybird Key Words Reading Scheme*. Each book told a different story in simple sentences using the same twenty words. Leslie read one of the books to him and then they read it together. Then Sam would try to read the book himself, asking for assistance when he needed it. Before long he could read it flawlessly. Leslie gave him the second book. He read it through immediately without hesitation. Sam had become a reader.

In all this, Sam was the leader. Leslie was emphatic about this. 'He pushed me along,' she said. It was his interest that initiated and sustained his development as a reader. It was Sam who started asking questions about print when he was barely three years old. He would examine the print on cereal boxes and milk cartons and ask about it. He listened with interest to the stories he was read, and then spontaneously made the link between the stories which had been read to him and the print on the page. He knew the stories off by heart and chose to spend time going through his books trying to work out what they said; trying to match his memory of the stories to the print on the page. He kept asking questions and Leslie kept answering them.

What Does Sam's Story Demonstrate About The Nature of Learning?

• Children actively seek to make sense of their world

If we draw conclusions about the nature of children's minds from what we know about Sam, there can be little doubt that children are indeed actively engaged in making sense of their world, including the print that is evident everywhere. It might be that Sam is extraordinary and should not be taken as an example of how the rest of plodding humanity thinks and learns, but we do not believe that this is the case. Sam has an active and enquiring mind, but that isn't exceptional. And he asked a lot of questions, but that's what three- and four-year-olds do.

Sam was unusual chiefly because he focused on print as something he especially wanted to understand. He asked his questions about print instead of badgering his parents about the tens of thousands of other things that little children identify as most interesting in their particular worlds. One thing is very clear, however. Sam's behaviour and achievements make it very difficult to believe that children learn only by being taught.

• Adults help children to understand the nature of desirable outcomes

There is no question that Leslie was involved in Sam's learning. Even though it had not been done with instructional intent, we can assume that it was because stories had been read to him from early in his life that he valued books as sources of pleasure and that he wanted to become a reader. He learnt what it meant to read a story. He learnt that not only could print represent spoken language but also that it 'stood for' particular language: the invariant language of the familiar story. On this basis he was able to adopt a plan of operation to help him read the books for himself. He tried to remember what the stories said and match it to the print in the books. He used what he already knew about books and reading to infer the rest.

• Adults support children's attempts to learn by responding to their interests and needs

When it became apparent that Sam was interested in print, Leslie took a more active part in his learning. She played 'I Spy' with him, thus directing his attention towards speech as something which could be analysed into words and sounds. This was not deliberate and systematic phonics instruction. She was simply responding to her son's interests and engaging him in enjoyable experiences which were related to those interests.

As Sam tried to read his books Leslie helped him again – but as respondent, not instructor. It was Sam who shaped these exchanges. He initiated the book-reading sessions. He decided what he needed to learn and he asked the questions. Leslie responded by not only answering his questions but also by urging him towards independence and withdrawing when he was able to proceed without her assistance. Like the effective teachers in the research studies cited here, Leslie's instructional intervention can best be described as 'leading by following'.

• Learning is a collaborative achievement

Leslie also intervened by simplifying and structuring the input of written language. She provided Sam with books with simple language structures and limited vocabulary and then read to him, and with him, until he had mastered one of the books. Then she withdrew again and gave him the freedom to think his way through the next book by himself.

Leslie and Sam illustrate the complementary roles of teacher and learner well. It would clearly be ludicrous to say that Sam learnt to read because he was taught. He is aptly described, in a phrase used by David Wood (1989, p.59) as the constructive architect of his own understanding. But Wood also says that children's efforts to understand are 'often enveloped within the more overarching competence of others'. Although Sam was the one who decided that he wanted to make sense of printed language, he needed Leslie's support. She helped him to think the problems through. She made understanding easier for him. But she did not teach him directly.

• Sam is seen to be a thinker

What Leslie believed about Sam's mind is wholly evident: she regarded him as a rational being, capable of making sense of written language. 'You got the last one,' she said. 'Try the next one. Think about it.'

Instead of trying to teach him to read, Leslie supported Sam in his efforts to understand written language. By answering his questions and reading with him she helped him to see how the things he had learnt on his own could be made part of a conventional understanding of how written language works and what it is used for. She helped him to understand how what he knew personally connected with what is known by the culture at large (Olson and Bruner, 1996). The incident involving Peter shows that Sam is still thinking about purposes for which written language can be used. It shows also that he understands that thinking and learning are not just individually pursued – they are often social, communicative and collaborative processes too.

Sam is by no means unique. In a study of thirty two children who started school at five able to read fluently, Margaret Clark (1976) comments

> It seems important not to ignore the evidence of children such as these ... and to appreciate that education neither begins at five years of age, nor at nine o'clock in the morning! We are all too ready to attribute the failures to the homes but to claim the entire success for the school and formal education. Any theory of reading is adequate only in as far as it takes account of children such as these.

This observation is sound. Sam makes learning to read look easy. Does this mean that, despite all assertions to the contrary, reading is not the complex and abstract process that Andrews, and Beard and Oakhill, and others say it is? Does it mean that reading can be easily mastered if we go about it in the right way? Does it mean, perhaps, that it is the experience of schooling that makes learning to read difficult for some children? These are questions that deserve attention. They certainly indicate that we should be devoting more time to trying to understand what successful learners like Sam do that makes learning seem so easy.

Thinking and Learning in Rhonda's Classroom

Early readers undoubtedly benefit from the presence of an adult who knows them intimately, answers their questions and gives them individual attention in every appropriate way. Moreover, it has been shown that formal educational settings do not provide the same opportunities for the negotiation of meaning through talk as exist in the home. It is also true that some researchers whose work we have cited in support of our argument have said that their results could not be expected to apply in a classroom. That is why the first half of this book provides a detailed description and analysis of two five-year-old girls learning to write in their first year of school – children who were not exceptional. The patterns of learning we described characterised how children learned in that class. What we have shown suggests that the broad principles of learning identified in studies of adult-child dyads can also apply to classroom learning in general and to learning to write specifically. The essential qualities of the learning we observed taking place in Rhonda Fisher's classroom are summed up below.

• The children learnt what it meant to 'write a story' in their classroom

This was achieved mainly by participation in joint story constructions. These occasions not only helped the children to understand what the desirable outcome was to be, but also provided a broad plan of action for achieving the outcome. They also presented opportunities for Rhonda to engage in 'strategic thinking aloud', something identified by Rogoff (1990) as an adult behaviour which contributes to children's learning.

• The children tried to produce written language texts from the earliest weeks of school

This is another aspect of the active participation in literacy activities which characterised Rhonda's classroom. Although the children could not yet write at the beginning of the year they were treated as if they were writers and they certainly did participate – but not, at first, by actually writing. During these sessions they did many things: copying classroom signs; writing strings of letters; writing lists of known words; drawing pictures. As time went on, they developed strategies for producing more satisfactory texts. They adopted topics Rhonda had used in writing her blackboard stories and used commonly known words which were available in the classroom to complete their stories.

It was also important that Rhonda, by asking the children to write, was letting them know implicitly that she believed that they were capable of working things out for themselves; that they did not need to be taught everything. These sessions gave the children opportunities to test their hypotheses about written language in a setting where they were free to experiment and could expect supportive feedback.

• The teacher responded contingently to the children's efforts to learn

David Wood has observed that the effectiveness of instruction depends upon the contingency of the tutor's responses to the learner. Generally, children clearly signal their lack of understanding. The effective tutor watches the children closely, always responding to whether they seem to understand what is expected of them. If a child seems unable to proceed the adult intervenes by offering more assistance. If the child understands what is required and is able to proceed independently, the adult withdraws and hands over control to the child. This accurately describes the way Rhonda responded to the children in her class. Although there was only one adult and many children, Rhonda frequently spoke to children individually or in small groups as they engaged in classroom tasks, and she always responded contingently in Wood's sense of the term during these exchanges.

• The children gradually accumulated a body of knowledge in common with the teacher about literacy and learning

In the first few months of the school year the children developed a range of experiences they shared with the other children and the teacher. These included participating in joint story construction, hearing books read; demonstrations of spelling rules; Big Book sessions;

discussions of the characteristics of print (eg. capital letters, apostrophes, full stops); and so on. These group experiences became a source of common knowledge the teacher used about writing. She guided the children in recalling relevant shared experiences and helped them to attend to aspects of those experiences which were relevant to the solution of problems the children encountered when writing their 'stories'.

• Although the teacher first acted as 'consciousness for two', helping the children to attend and remember, they gradually learned to direct their own attention and cue their own memories

Rhonda rarely answered questions directly. She consistently responded to requests for information by asking the children where they might find the answers to their own questions and providing clues to assist in the recall and recognition of required words. In time the children began to cue their own memories and to direct their own attention using the cues of the kind that Rhonda had originally provided. In this way the mental processes were brought under voluntary control through the use of language.

Grapho-phonemic correspondences were also dealt with in this way. When the children discovered a need to use specific words in their writing, Rhonda would often remind them about a previous experience of having seen the word and having discussed how it was spelled, or of an occasion when a relevant spelling generalization had been demonstrated. Their ultimate control of spelling depended not on drills or practices but on learning to remember the relevant discussion or demonstration.

• In classrooms like this much of the learning proceeds through conversational exchanges in which the child negotiates meanings with the teacher

The establishment of joint attention is basic to achieving mutual understanding and is managed through conversation. Only when both teacher and child are focused on the same thing can the talk in the situation be reliably interpreted. If learning is to occur, however, the dialogue must continue, so the teacher's primary aim was to maintain the conversation until mutually satisfactory outcomes were reached. The prominence of conversational exchanges as a means of learning distinguished this classroom from many others. The implied assumption underlying Rhonda's approach to instruction is that knowledge cannot be transmitted directly from adult to child but must instead arise from a collaborative construction of knowledge (Wells and Chang-Wells, 1992). Most of the episodes described showed Rhonda engaged in such collaboration with the children, helping them to negotiate meanings and fine-tune their knowledge of literacy.

• The children were encouraged to help each other to attend and remember so that a collective consciousness was developed in the group
Rhonda often invoked the collective consciousness of the class. If the child who asked the question could not recall the relevant incident, Rhonda usually drew other children into the act of remembering. This became part of the routine of the class, with children frequently using not only the physical environment of the class, but also the collective memory and knowledge of the group as a resource for solving written language problems.

Becoming Literate: Making Connections
Learning in Rhonda's class was social and collaborative and involved the joint negotiation of meanings through conversational exchanges. To promote learning the teacher involved the children in collective thinking and joint decision-making in the context of literacy activities. Understanding depended upon the growth of common knowledge through joint action and talk (Edwards and Mercer, 1987, 1989). As the children became more competent, the teacher handed control to them so they could proceed independently in the further development of their competence as writers.

This book has examined methods of instruction and ways of learning but has also drawn attention to what children learn as they become literate. Learning to be literate is complex – but possibly in ways other than those suggested by Andrews (1992). Becoming literate should involve learning the potential uses of reading and writing; learning how to find out about what others know and believe, and comparing it with ones's own knowledge; developing an awareness of being part of a continuing tradition of reading and writing; and learning that literacy provides new ways of thinking. Literacy learning should produce confident, independent self-regulating learners who learn a little more every time they read and every time they write. Moreover, these things are not learnt sequentially. From the first day at school children should begin to learn simultaneously about literacy and learning, and about themselves as learners, and about the things that can be done with reading and writing. Highly structured, teacher-controlled programmes are likely to develop in children only a limited conception of literacy and a limiting view of themselves as learners.

Thinking About Literacy and Learning

Becoming literate, like all other learning, is also a matter of learning about yourself. This book has sought to shift the focus of attention away from the discussion of methods of teaching children to be literate towards a consideration of how children learn, because the teachers' beliefs about learning are primary. How we teach is derived from what we believe about how children learn. If, for example, we believe that children must be taught in order to learn, and that the matter of central importance is the development of automaticity of response, then instruction is likely to involve much in the way of teacher-directed drills and practices. And even if children find those drills and practices enjoyable they will be little more than passive participants in adult-controlled activities.

Our beliefs about learning influence how we teach. How we teach, in turn, influences the children's views of themselves as learners. If our approach to instruction is to engage children in shared thinking and joint decision-making, and if we encourage them to seek their own solutions to problems, then they will learn that they are not dependent on instruction. There is a good chance that they will become independent thinkers and confident problem-solvers. Such children will always learn more than they are being taught.

In Chapter Six we wrote about Jenny, a child whose experience of learning to read and write had convinced her that there was a fixed 'right' way and 'wrong' way to read and write. She wanted her teacher to tell her explicitly how to complete her writing project so that she could be sure of getting a good grade for it. This was a child whose experience of schooling had limited her capacity to learn. She had learnt that she needed to be told exactly what to do, and that the ultimate mark of success was the grade she was given. Fortunately, in Hazel's class, she was being given a second chance.

Lucy, the child in Chapter Eight, was different. She had a positive view of herself as a learner and thinker and also a clear conception of how she wanted people to help her to learn. In her home she had been encouraged to solve her own problems and to defend the decisions she made, so she often irritated her teachers by asking them for reasons and justifications. Her parents had taught her to regard writing as a way of thinking, and she was a confident and proficient writer. But her experience of schooling had disappointed her. Instead of being allowed to use language to explore possibilities, she mostly had to write what the teachers wanted. Pressure to conform threatened not only to undermine her confidence in herself as a writer but to force upon her the school's limiting definition of herself as a learner. Unlike Jenny, however, Lucy's conception of herself as capable of thinking problems through and finding solutions was very strong. She did not abandon her belief in herself as a thinker and learner.

Learning to be Literate: Making Contact With the Literate Tradition

Becoming literate is also a matter of making contact with the culture of literacy and, beyond that, with the broader culture in which you are learning. Although she was only eleven years old, Lucy knew (though perhaps not explicitly in every detail) that learning was a social and cultural matter. She was aware that she needed to be able to talk to more expert others about her writing. She wanted her teachers to 'show her what good writing was like' and challenge her to think about ways of using what she already knew to find solutions to her writing problems, just as her parents had.

Lucy had developed the practice, again cultivated by her parents, of constantly comparing what she was writing with what she had previously read. Just as the parents in David Wood's studies (Wood and Middleton, 1975; Wood, Bruner and Ross, 1976; Wood, 1980) assisted their four-year-olds to construct wooden models which they could not build by themselves, so did Lucy's parents help her to think about books and writing in ways that opened up paths of development that might otherwise not have been followed. The puzzles Lucy learnt to solve, however, had no fixed solutions. They arose from her efforts after meaning; her attempts to find ways of saying exactly what she wanted to say. And instead of being taught to look for the single available solution, Lucy learnt to consider options.

Only one teacher gave her the same support her parents offered. He showed her how other people, at other times and in other places, had set out to overcome writing problems not unlike the ones which confronted her. He provided her with examples of how skilled writers had bridged the gap between the meanings we hold in our heads and their expression on the page. He helped her to make the connection between her personal knowledge about writing and what others knew. He helped her to position herself as a writer in relation to other writers in a tradition of writing.

Her learning, however, did not consist of simple imitation of past models. Like her parents, this teacher insisted that she did all the thinking. He presented her with possibilities but insisted that she make decisions for herself. He helped her to learn in much the same way as Rhonda and Hazel and Ruth helped the children in their classes by involving them in shared thinking and joint problem-solving. He supported her when she needed help and then stepped back and let her proceed independently once she could.

Far too many teachers are not writers in any but the most superficial sense. They have never struggled, as Lucy has, with trying to express the inexpressible. They do not know about the drudgery of writing and the relief of getting the job finished. They do not know that writing, as much as music or art, exists in a tradition of its own which is a resource for generating meanings. They have never used writing as a way of exploring possibilities or reflecting upon their lives. They do not really understand what it means to be a writer. How, then, could they be expected to help children like Lucy to grow as writers? How, indeed, could they be expected to help any child to become a truly literate adult? Until every teacher thoroughly understands literacy, until each one is a voracious and insatiable reader, and a practised and thoughtful writer, we will continue to fail the children we teach. Lucy has told us clearly what children need as literacy learners. It is up to teachers to meet the challenge she presents.

The Final Word

In the 1970s Barbara Tizard and Martin Hughes used radio micro-phones to collect extensive samples of children talking to their mothers at home and their teachers at nursery school. Analysis of their data suggested that it was the home which provided the more linguistically and intellectually stimulating environment. Adult-child conversations were fewer and briefer at school, and teachers contributed far more to conversations than did mothers. At home the contributions of adult and child were more balanced.

Tizard and Hughes characterise three and four-year -olds as 'puzzlers', and the most obvious manifestation of the puzzling minds of children, they say, is the questions they ask. Their results showed that at home children asked their mothers an average of twenty-six questions an hour. At school they asked their teachers an average of two questions per hour. Conversations at home quite often included what Tizard and Hughes call 'passages of intellectual search' – episodes in which the child persistently questioned an adult in pursuit of new information or explanations, or to make sense of apparent anomalies in their experience of the world. Such 'passages of intellectual search' were totally missing from the conversations at school. Had children been judged by their conversations at school, their capacity as thinkers and learners would have seemed limited. But Tizard and Hughes make the following observation about children's conversations with their mothers at home:

> Our analysis of the conversations at home led us to an enhanced respect for the intellectual activities of four-year-olds. Although the home pro-vides a very powerful learning environment, children are by no means passive absorbers or recipients of the environment. On the contrary, their own intellectual efforts are an essential part of the learning process. Even with the most attentive mothers this process was not always easy. In all the homes many questions went unanswered, much was left im-plicit, misunderstandings were often undetected by the mothers, full explanations were rarely given, and many explanations were definitely

misleading. Armed only with their curiosity, logic and persistence, the children tackled the task of making sense of a world they imperfectly understood. (Tizard and Hughes, 1984, p.253)

Leslie did not have time to answer adequately all the questions Sam asked about print or to provide regular, systematic instruction for him even if she had wanted to do so. She certainly helped him to learn about print but his development as a reader had its origins in his own curiosity about written language, and his eventual success depended upon his persistence in trying to make sense of it. He *wanted* to be able to read so he sat, day after day, remembering the words of the stories he knew and trying to find them on the page in front of him until he could make sense of his books. And when he could not proceed on his own he asked his mother questions. His learning was driven by his private intellectual efforts but he also needed the support of other people who were willing and able to try to answer the questions he asked.

His persistent curiosity about the world was not, however, limited to an interest in reading. One day when he was five, Leslie took him to the local Leisure Centre for a swim. She was helping him change when he said, 'What are we here for mummy?'

Leslie was puzzled.

'You know what we're here for Sam. We're getting changed so we can go for a swim.'

'No,' said Sam. 'I mean on this earth.'

Sam may have the makings of a philosopher about him, but we know he is not exceptional. Tizard and Hughes (1984) tell us that their analysis of discussions between children and their mothers showed that '... young children's interests extend to any aspect of life that impinges on them – the neighbours, money, electric lights, the structure and arrangement of houses, parent's work, God, the death of pets, doctors' (p.261). Leslie was intrigued by Sam's question but not surprised. She *knew* that he was always likely to ask her more significant questions than she would think to ask him. Sam's questions helped Leslie to know where his enquiring mind was seeking to go. They revealed what he already knew, what he was currently thinking about and how she could best help him to make sense of things. This is why children's questions are so important to those who help children learn. They provide clear indications of what children are ready to learn *with assistance*. They mark each child's zones of proximal development. They help us to identify and foster the growth of 'ripening functions'.

But evidence suggests that Sam would have been unlikely to ask the same question of a teacher. In school he would probably have had neither the inclination nor the opportunity to enquire about the reasons for human existence on our planet. In many classrooms opportunities to learn are limited by the fact that child-initiated questions are rare. This book shows that it is possible to create classrooms in which children ask many questions and routinely solve problems in cooperation with other people. Learning proceeds more smoothly in these classrooms because communication is genuinely reciprocal. Knowledge is collaboratively constructed and problem-solving is jointly achieved.

Jerome Bruner has written about the changes that gradually occurred in his understanding of the nature of learning. Bruner (1986) says that his conception early in his career of the child as learner had been 'very much in the tradition of the solo child mastering the world by representing it to himself in his own terms'. In the intervening years, he says

> I have come increasingly to recognise that most learning in most settings is a communal activity, a sharing of the culture. It is not just that the child must make his knowledge his own, but that he must make it in a community of those who share his sense of belonging to a culture. It is this that leads me to emphasise not only discovery and invention but the importance of negotiating and sharing – in a word, of joint culture creating as an object of schooling and as an appropriate step *en route* to becoming a member of the adult society in which one lives out one's life. (p.127)

The authors of this book have trodden much the same path in their efforts to find an adequate explanation of the nature of learning. Consequently they see Sam and Hannelore and Emma and Kim and Karen and Lucy as Piagetian children: lone scientists testing hypotheses formed on the basis of their own representations of reality. But they also see them as Vygotskian children for whom learning is, as Bruner puts it, a communal activity carried on within a cultural framework. They see them as collaborative problem-solvers whose thinking involves a sharing of consciousness: collective remembering, shared decision-making, joint reasoning and so on.

Other people involved in literacy education have chosen different paths. Beard and Oakhill, for example, reject the notion that children can discover for themselves the alphabetic principle underlying written language. But not adding Vygotsky's conception of learning as an essentially social and cultural process to Piaget's conception of children as active constructors of their own knowledge, they have replaced the notion of the child as 'lone scientist' with that of the child as 'information processor'. And information-processing children do not engage in the negotiation of meaning. Nor do they engage in collective remembering or other collaborative acts of thought. Beard and Oakhill's children are asocial encoders and retrievers of information who must be taught, because without explicit instruction they are unlikely to learn.

The limitations of teaching must, however, be acknowledged if progress is to be made in improving literacy programmes. Teaching often fails but children never cease to learn. In our years of observation in many classrooms we have been surprised constantly by what children know and can do. Successful learners always go beyond what they have been taught. But children can be confused by adults who make them feel that they are poor learners and are dependent on instruction. And even when they gain some control over reading and writing they often fail to understand where literacy is connected to their lives or their culture, or that it can be used as a way of reflecting on experience and solving problems.

We must have faith in the power of children's minds, in their ability to learn independently. That does not mean that the teacher's role is to be a mere facilitator of learning. Teachers are instructors but the instruction they provide must be sensitively related to the children's efforts to learn. The teacher's most important functions are to demonstrate what the outcomes of learning might be and, even before children are able to participate fully, to engage them in goal-directed culturally significant activities. Then, while the children are participating at whatever level they can manage, the adult should listen; pay attention; hear the questions; understand the problems; intervene to remove obstacles and smooth the way so that learning can take place. Follow where the children lead. The solution to the problem of how to improve literacy instruction, as we have shown in this book, is as simple – and as complicated – as that.

Bibliography

Adams, M. J. (1994) Modelling the connections between word recognition and reading. In Ruddell, R., Rapp Ruddell, M. and Singer, H. (eds.) *Theoretical Models and Processes of Reading* (fourth edition). Newark, Del.: International Reading Association.

Andrews, S. (1992) A skills approach: optimising initial reading instruction. In Watson, A. and Badenhop, A (eds.). *Prevention of Reading Failure*. Sydney: Ashton Scholastic.

Ashton-Warner, S. (1980) *Teacher*. London: Virago.

Baker, C. and Luke, A. (eds.). (1991) *Towards a Critical Sociology of Reading Pedagogy: Papers of the XII World Congress on Reading*. Amsterdam: John Benjamins.

Beard, R. and Oakhill, J. (1994) *Reading By Apprenticeship? A Critique of the 'Apprenticeship Approach' to the Teaching of Reading*. Slough: National Federation for Educational Research.

Bremer, K., Roberts, C., Vaseur, M., Simonot, M. and Broeder, P. (1996) *Achieving Understanding: Discourse in Inter-Cultural Encounters*. London: Longman.

Brown, R. (1980) The maintenance of conversation. In Olson. D. (ed.) *The Social Foundations of Language and Thought*. London: Norton.

Bruner, J. (1983) *Child's Talk: Learning to Use Language*. Oxford: Oxford University Press.

Bruner, J. (1986) *Actual Minds, Possible Worlds*. Cambridge, Mass: Harvard University Press.

Bruner, J. and Haste, H. (eds.) (1987) *Making Sense: the Child's Construction of the World*. London: Methuen.

Cambourne, B.L. (1988) *The Whole Story: Natural Learning and the Acquisition of Literacy in the Classroom*. Sydney: Ashton Scholastic.

Cambourne, B.L. (1995) Toward an educationally relevant theory of literacy learning: Twenty years of inquiry. *The Reading Teacher*, 49, 3, 182-190.

Clark, M. (1976) *Young Fluent Readers*. London: Heinemann.

Clay, M. (1987) Learning to be learning disabled. *New Zealand Journal of Educational Studies*, 22, 2, 155-173.

Cook-Gumperz, J. (1975) The child as practical reasoner. In Sanches, M. and Blount, B. (eds.) *Sociocultural Dimensions of Language Use*. New York: Academic Press.

Cook-Gumperz, J. (ed.) (1986) *The Social Construction of Literacy*. Cambridge: Cambridge University Press.

Edwards, D. and Mercer, N. (1987) *Common Knowledge: The Development of Common Knowledge in the Classroom*. London: Methuen.

Edwards, D. and Mercer, N. (1989) Reconstructing context: the conventionalization of classroom knowledge. *Discourses Processes*, 12, 91-104.

Evans, R. (1993) Learning schooled literacy: The literate life histories of mainstream student readers and writers. *Discourse Processes*, 16, 317-340.

Flavell, J., Miller, P. and Miller, S. (1993) *Cognitive Development* (third edition). Englewood Cliffs, N.J.: Prentice-Hall.

Funnell, E. and Stuart, M. (eds.) (1995) *Learning to Read: Psychology in the Classroom*. Oxford: Blackwell.

Gaffney, J. and Anderson, R. C. (1991) Two-tiered scaffolding: congruent processes of teaching and learning. In Hiebert, E. (ed.) *Literacy for a Diverse Society: Perspectives, Practices and Policies*. Teachers College Press: New York.

Geekie, P. and Raban, B. (1994) Language learning at home and school. In Gallaway, C. and Richards, B. *Input and Interaction in Language Acquisition*. Cambridge: Cambridge University Press.

Geekie, P. and Raban, B. (1993) *Learning to Read and Write Through Classroom Talk*. Stoke on Trent: Trentham Books.

Green, J. and Meyer, L. (1991) The embeddedness of reading in classroom life: reading as a situated process. In Baker, C. and Luke, A. (eds.) *Towards a Critical Sociology of Reading Pedagogy: Papers of the XII World Congress on Reading*. Amsterdam: John Benjamins.

Gumperz, J. (1982) *Discourse Strategies*. Cambridge: Cambridge University Press.

Hughes, T. (1976) Myth and education, in Fox, G., Hammond, G., Jones, T., Smith, F. and Sterck, K. (eds.) *Writers, Critics and Children*. London: Heinemann.

Lloyd, P. (1990) Children's communication. In Grieve, R. and Hughes, M. (eds.) *Understanding Children*. Oxford: Blackwell.

Lloyd, P. (1991) Strategies used to convey route directions by telephone: a comparison of the performance of 7-year-olds, 10-year-olds and adults. *Journal of Child Language*, 18, 171-189.

Lloyd, P. (1992) New directions in referential communication research. *British Journal of Developmental Psychology*, 10, 385-403.

Lloyd, P. (1993) Referential communication as teaching: adults tutoring their own and other children. *First Language*, 13, 339-357.

Lucariello, J. and Nelson, K. (1985) Slot-filler categories as memory organisers for young children. *Developmental Psychology*, 21, 272-282.

Mackay, D., Thompson, B., and Schaub, P. (1970) *Breakthrough To Literacy Teacher's Manual: The Theory and Practice of Teaching Initial Reading and Writing*. London: Longman.

Martin, Bill Jr. (1972) *The Sounds of Language Readers*. New York: Holt, Rinehart and Winston.

Murray, D. (1975) On the Work of Writers. Course materials at the University of New Hampshire.

Nelson, K and Gruendel, J. (1986) Children's scripts. In K. Nelson (ed.) *Event Knowledge: Structure and Function in Development*. Hillsdale, N. J.: Erlbaum.

Olson, D. (1986) Learning to mean what you say: toward a psychology of literacy. In de Castell, S., Luke, A. and Egan, K. *Literacy, Society and Schooling*. Cambridge: Cambridge University Press.

Olson, D. (1991) Literacy as metalinguistic activity. In Olson, D. and Torrance, N. (ed.) *Literacy and Orality*. Cambridge: Cambridge University Press.

Olson, D. (1996) *The World on Paper: The Conceptual and Cognitive Implications of Writing and Reading*. Cambridge: Cambridge University Press.

Olson, D. and Bruner, J. (1996) Folk psychology and folk pedagogy. In Olson, D. and Torrance, N. *The Handbook of Education and Human Development: New Models of Learning, Teaching and Schooling*. Cambridge, Mass.: Blackwell.

Olson, D. and Torrance, N. (1987) Language, literacy and mental states. *Discourse Processes*, 10, 157-167.

Radziszewska, B. and Rogoff, B. (1988) Influence of adult and peer collaborators on children's planning skills. *Developmental Psychology*, 24, 840-848.

Robinson, E., Goelman, H. and Olson, D. (1983) Children's understanding of the relation between expressions (what was said) and intentions (what was meant). *British Journal of Developmental Psychology*, 1, 75-86.

Robinson, E. and Robinson, W. (1985) Teaching children about verbal referential communication. *International Journal of Behavioral Development*, 8, 285-299.

Robinson, E. and Whittaker, S. (1987a) Learning about verbal referential communication in the early school years. In Durkin, K. (ed.) *Language Development in the School Years*. London: Croom Helm.

Robinson, E. and Whittaker, S. (1987b) Children's conception of relations between messages, meanings and reality. *British Journal of Developmental Psychology*, 5, 81-90.

Rogoff, B. (1989) The joint socialization of development by young children and adults. In Gellatly, A., Rogers, D. and Sloboda, J. *Cognition and Social Worlds*. Oxford: The Clarendon Press.

Rogoff, B. (1990) *Apprenticeship in Thinking: Cognitive Development in Social Context.* Oxford: Oxford University Press.

Rogoff, B. (1991) Social interaction as apprenticeship in thinking: guidance and participation in spatial planning. In Resnick, L., Levine, J. and Teasley, S. (ed.) *Perspectives on Socially Shared Cognition.*Washington: American Psychological Association.

Rogoff, B., Matusov, E. and White, C. (1996) Models of teaching and learning: participation in a community of learners. In Olson, D. and Torrance, N. *The Handbook of Education and Human Development: New Models of Learning, Teaching and Schooling.* Cambridge, Mass.: Blackwell.

Rogoff, B and Toma, C. (1997) Shared thinking: community and institutional variations. *Discourse Processes,* 23, 471-497.

Ruddell, R., Rapp Ruddell, M. and Singer, H. (eds.) (1994) *Theoretical Models and Processes of Reading* (fourth edition). Newark, Del.: International Reading Association.

Smith, F. (1981) *Essays Into Literacy.* London: Heinemann.

Tierney, R., Readence, J., and Dishner, E. (1980) *Reading Strategies and Practices: A Guide For Improving Instruction.* Boston, Mass: Allyn and Bacon.

Tizard, B. and Hughes, M. (1984) *Young Children Learning: Talking and Thinking at Home and at School.* London: Fontana.

Van Der Veer, R. and Valsiner, J. (eds.) (1994) *The Vygotsky Reader.* Oxford: Blackwell.

Vygotsky, L. (1978.) *Mind in Society: The Development of the Higher Psychological Processses.* Cambridge, Mass.:Harvard University Press.

Vygotsky, L. (1986) *Thought and Language.* Cambridge, Mass.: The MIT Press.

Waterland, L. (1988) *Read With Me: An Apprenticeship Approach to Reading* (second edition). Stroud: Thimble Press.

Watson, A. and Badenhop, A (eds.). (1992) *Prevention of Reading Failure.* Sydney: Ashton Scholastic.

Wells, G. (1981) *Learning Through Interaction.* Cambridge: Cambridge University Press.

Wells, G. (1985) *Language Development in the Pre-School Years.* Cambridge: Cambridge University Press.

Wells, G. (1986) *The Meaning Makers: Children Learning Language and Using Language to Learn.* Portsmouth, N.H.: Heinemann.

Wells, G. and Chang-Wells, G.L. (1992) *Constructing Knowledge Together: Classrooms as Centres of Inquiry and Literacy.* Portsmouth, NH: Heinemann.

Wertsch, James V. (1983) The role of semiosis in L. S. Vygotsky's theory of human cognition. In Bruce Bain (ed.). *The Sociogenesis of Language and Human Conduct.* New York: Plenum Press.

Wood, D. (1980) Teaching the young child: some relationships between social inter-action, language, and thought. In Olson. D. (ed.) *The Social Foundations of Language and Thought*. London: Norton.

Wood, D. (1988a) *How Children Think and Learn*. Oxford: Blackwell.

Wood, D. (1988b) Aspects of teaching and learning. In Richards, M. and Light, P. (ed.) *Children of Social Worlds; Development in a Social Context*. Oxford: Polity Press. p.199

Wood, D. (1989) Social interaction as tutoring In Bornstein, M. and Bruner, J. *Interaction in Human Development*. Hillsdale, N.J.: Lawrence Erlbaum.

Wood, D., Bruner, J. and Ross, G. (1976) The role of tutoring in problem solving. *Journal of Child Psychology and Psychiatry*, 17, 2, 89-100.

Wood, D. and Middleton, D. (1975) A study of assisted problem solving. *British Journal of Psychology*, 66, 2, 181-191.

INDEX